The Foreign Policy of Self-Interest:
A Moral Ideal for America

by Peter Schwartz

AYN RAND
INSTITUTE PRESS

Ayn Rand Institute Press
Copyright © 2004 by Peter Schwartz

First printing May 2004
10 9 8 7 6 5 4 3 2 1

http://www.aynrand.org/

ISBN: 0-9625336-6-1

Production by Simon Federman
Cover design by Michael Chiavaroli

The Moral Foundations of Public Policy:
a series from the Ayn Rand Institute

In the weeks, months and now years since September 11, one crucial lesson has yet to be widely understood. The chief cause of our vulnerability to such horrific attacks was not a failure of the intelligence community, but a failure in our basic approach to foreign policy—an approach that is incapable of eliminating the threats posed by America's enemies.

Critics of our foreign policy abound. Some cite tactical military blunders, while others lament diplomatic mistakes in this or that particular conflict. But the problem is far deeper. Foreign policy is neither a starting point nor a self-contained field. It is, rather, the product of certain ideas in political and moral philosophy. Without a solid foundation, no house can remain standing for long; similarly, without a rational intellectual base, no foreign policy can be effective in safeguarding the nation. Indeed, for precisely that reason, America's foreign policy has been an unmitigated disaster for decades. It has failed because of the bankrupt moral philosophy our political leaders have chosen to accept: the philosophy of altruism and self-sacrifice.

This book offers the intellectual foundation for a radically different foreign policy—one based on self-interest as a moral ideal. The building blocks of that foundation come from Ayn Rand's philosophic system, Objectivism, which espouses the values of reason, individualism and capitalism.

Demonstrating the inescapable role of philosophy in politics, this volume is the first in a planned series from the Ayn Rand Institute on the proper moral foundations of public policy.

—Dr. Yaron Brook
Executive Director, Ayn Rand Institute
Spring 2004

Table of Contents

The Basic Alternatives

What explains a foreign policy under which the strongest nation on earth regularly allows itself to be thwarted by petty despots? America wages a putative War on Terror, while Iran—the world's most active state-sponsor of terrorism, the patron of the terrorist group that is second only to al Qaeda in the number of Americans it has slaughtered, the theocracy that stormed our embassy and held fifty-two Americans captive for over a year as its ayatollahs' minions pranced in the streets and chanted "Death to America"—escapes any military reprisal from us.

We insist that we will not tolerate nuclear weapons in the hands of totalitarian North Korea—yet we permit its nuclear facilities to remain intact and pay it protection money for a decade in exchange for its promise not to utilize those facilities. And when its ruler boasts of having abrogated the agreement, we respond, not by military action, but by demurring to a demand for additional protection money—until Pyongyang agrees to include other nations in the negotiations about the specifics of the payments.

China forces down a U.S. reconnaissance plane in international air space and holds its crew captive for eleven days—yet we not only apologize for having flown the plane, but after the Chinese insist on dismantling the aircraft, we "reimburse" them for the costs of taking it apart and shipping it back to us.

Multi-billions in U.S. foreign aid are doled out to countries that excoriate us as corrupt hegemonists. America is routinely vilified at the United Nations, while we blandly continue to provide the financial and political support which makes the existence of that dictatorship-laden body possible.

Why? Why do we allow our enemies to act against us with such impunity? Why are we reluctant to stand up to other nations, when we enjoy undisputed military superiority? There is certainly no physical impediment that keeps us from protecting America's interests. There is, however, an intellectual one: the widely accepted idea that *the pursuit of self-interest is morally tainted.*

The premise shaping our foreign policy is that we must sacrifice ourselves for the sake of weaker nations because self-interest cannot be the standard of our actions. Thus, if Africa needs money to deal with a medical crisis, America provides it. If Mexico needs another massive loan—America arranges it. If China needs nuclear technology—America furnishes it. If troops are needed in Kosovo to separate murderous ethnic clans, or in Somalia to neutralize some local warlord, or in Liberia to interpose themselves among the factions of a civil war—America sends them.

Policymakers differ on the type of assistance to be provided, with liberals and conservatives arguing over whether it should be primarily economic or military in nature. But that is a dispute only about form. On the substantive question of whether another nation's need, for food or for weapons, creates a moral duty on our part to fulfill it, all parties answer affirmatively. They may at times invoke spurious claims of national self-interest to justify pouring American resources down a bottomless foreign-aid pit, but the true rationale is always the altruistic injunction to think of others before ourselves.

This is why our government does not respond self-assertively and unapologetically to all foreign threats. We don't want to focus only on our own security. We want to accommodate the concerns of the international community. We don't want to use force "unilaterally" against nations that pose dangers to us—we have to consider their needs too. So we can't tell the North Koreans that if they don't destroy their nuclear-weapons facilities, we will; we must sympathize with their point of view. We can't demand that Syria stop running terrorist training camps; we must respect its political needs. We can't punish China for downing our aircraft; we must resolve all conflicts through compromise. After all, the North Koreans or the Syrians or the Chinese may have their own complaints against America.

The precept of self-sacrifice pertains not only to material goods, but to intellectual assets as well. Just as you are urged to hand over your money for the sake of others, so you are urged to surrender your *convictions* in the cause of altruism. Who are you to insist self-righteously on the truth of your viewpoint?—this precept demands. What about your opponent's viewpoint? Isn't one man's terrorist another man's freedom-fighter? You can't condemn any countries as part of an "axis of evil"; they probably think the same of you. Never believe that you know the truth—that is too self-confident. Never decide on your own to resort to force against other nations—that is too self-assured. Be flexible, negotiate, give in, give up.

The result of these admonitions is a U.S. foreign policy whose hallmark is self-doubt.

While we do at times take military action in our defense, it is usually perfunctory, intended only to slap the offender on the wrist. The Clinton administration's 1996 bombing of a Sudanese pharmaceutical factory and an empty Afghani camp, in response to al Qaeda's deadly strike against two U.S. embassies in Africa, was typical (though that reprisal missed even the offender's wrist). Worst of all, we refuse to take action to *prevent* disaster. For example, regarding the basic threat posed by al Qaeda, there is nothing we learned on September 11, 2001, that we did not know years earlier. When our government knows about an Osama bin Laden who in 1998 declared a "holy war" in which Muslims were ordered to execute every American they could—a bin Laden whose al Qaeda organization has launched various attacks that have killed Americans since at least 1993—a bin Laden who was indicted by federal grand juries in 1996 and in 1998 for three such attacks—a bin Laden who has been on the FBI's list of Ten Most Wanted Fugitives since 1999—and a bin Laden whose terrorist activities are being sustained since 1996 by the government of Afghanistan—with all this information, the principle of self-interest should have mandated the forcible elimination of the Afghani regime, and of al Qaeda, well before September 11. But that principle is precisely what is absent among our self-doubting policymakers.

Invading a sovereign state—they feared—would have been selfish "unilateralism" on our part. Prior to the international support generated, temporarily, by September 11, Washington would not tolerate such drastic action. Who are we to kill others just because we think they threaten us? Shouldn't we have some empathy for people living in desperate straits? How can we ignore the world's disapproval? Shouldn't we try more diplomacy, so that both sides can air their grievances? And if that means increasing the risk to us—our policymakers cautioned—well, we can't be so parochially consumed with our own problems.

This attitude is what explains the bizarre phenomenon of a military power being paralyzed by a patently weaker opponent, whose arsenal consists essentially of the disarming idea that the strong must sacrifice to the weak.

But there is an alternative to this self-inflicted impotence: a foreign policy based on self-interest. This is a foreign policy that views the protection of Americans against international threats as its all-encompassing goal. The advocates of such a policy would reject any duty to sacrifice the wealth and the lives of Americans to the needs of other nations. And they would not seek the approval of other countries before deciding to use force to guard America's interests. Under such a foreign policy, Washington would not attempt to defend America in fits and starts, futilely trying to straddle the two roads of self-interest and self-sacrifice, attacking one terror-sponsor today while mollifying others the next day. Nor would it attempt to uphold self-interest as an amoral expediency—as advocated by the impractical pragmatists and their school of *realpolitik*. Rather, the designers of a rational foreign policy would understand that self-interest can be successfully defended only if it is embraced as a consistent, *moral* principle—a principle in keeping with America's founding values.

America is based on the recognition of each individual's right to life, liberty and the pursuit of happiness. This means that the government may not treat the citizen as a serf—i.e., as someone who exists to serve the needs of others. Rather, each individual is a free, sovereign entity, entitled to live his own life for his own sake, no matter how loudly some people may wail about their need for his services. That is the meaning of inalienable rights. If a foreign aggressor threatens the rights of Americans, our government safeguards those rights by wielding retaliatory force so that its citizens can remain free—free to purse the goals they have chosen to further their own lives.

Those rights, however, are vitiated by a foreign policy of self-sacrifice. When we send our armed forces into a country that poses a physical threat to Americans, each of those soldiers is fighting to defend his own interests. But when we send them to be altruistic "peacekeepers" in countries that do not threaten U.S. security, we are telling those soldiers to risk their lives in self-abnegating servitude to others. Similarly, when we fail to use military means to remove a danger to Americans—when the danger is allowed to persist because we want to subordinate our interests to the demands of the global community—then, too, we are sacrificing the citizen's rights. Only a foreign policy that holds self-interest as its moral purpose is consistent with America's founding principle of liberty.

This leads to the crucial question of what actually *constitutes* America's interests. The answer that State Department officials habitually offer amounts to: "There can be no confining rules about our interests; we have to go by whatever feels right at the time." This is why even when they are trying to protect this country's interests, they fail dismally. Our policymakers lack an objective standard by which to judge whether a course of action does or does not advance America's interests.

In her system of ethics, Ayn Rand presented not only a validation of self-interest as man's moral purpose, but also an analysis of what man's self-interest entails. She demonstrated that one's self-interest is achieved, not by "instinct" or by whim, but by acting in accord with the factual requirements of man's life, which means: by living as a rational being. Since the concept of self-interest pertains fundamentally to the individual, the idea of a nation's self-interest refers only to the political precondition of a person's living rationally in a social setting, which means: freedom. Without freedom, man cannot pursue the values his life demands. Just as in ethics it is maintaining his own life that should be the individual's ultimate purpose, in politics it is maintaining its own citizens' liberty that should be the government's ultimate purpose. Not the pragmatic, amoral goal of preserving a "balance of power" or of establishing "spheres of influence"—but the moral goal of keeping Americans free. Freedom is the end to which all other political actions are the means. *This* is the standard by which a nation's interests ought to be measured—and this is where the science of foreign policy should begin.

And this is the standard that would differentiate our foreign policy from that of a dictatorship. When people assert that a foreign policy based solely on protecting the United States against attack is devoid of moral content because, they say, even a totalitarian state employs its armies to defend its interests—they are ignoring this standard. They are dropping the context within which a nation's self-interest is defined. Keeping a leash around people's necks cannot be in their interests—but in a dictatorship the armed forces serve as that leash. Their function is to help maintain the condition of enslavement. In a free country, the military shields its citizens from subjugation. In a totalitarian state, however, it shields against the opposite. What the armies of a Nazi Germany, a Soviet Russia or a Taliban government in Afghanistan shield the citizen from is: liberation. Their armies keep their people in thrall. A dictatorship's foreign policy is essentially the same as its domestic policy. Both are intended not—as America's are—to uphold the citizen's rights, but to abrogate them. And what both achieve, therefore, is not self-interest but self-destruction. Only a nation that enshrines freedom can adopt a foreign policy that is actually based on self-interest.

Since freedom can be breached only by the initiation of force, our foreign policy must protect us from foreign aggressors. Our government must safeguard American lives and property by using retaliatory force against the initiators. This is how our freedom is preserved.

It is true that the rise of freedom anywhere in the world benefits us. It eliminates potential enemies, it creates new allies in securing our own freedom against militaristic dictatorships and it generates new sources of economic production and trade. Consequently—the State Department's dogmatic worship of "stability" notwithstanding—we should always give moral support to any people who are fighting for freedom against an oppressive government. But this does not mean we ought to declare war on every tyrant in the world. Before we decide to wage war, there must exist a serious threat to our own freedom. Our government is not the world's policeman.

It is, however, *America's* policeman. And that job is primarily an intellectual undertaking. A heavily armed military is useless when backed by an ideologically disarmed State Department. It was not the military superiority of the enemy that compelled U.S. troops to flee Vietnam in 1975—or that allowed Iran to capture our embassy in 1979—or that caused the Marines to retreat from Lebanon in 1983—or that drove American soldiers from Somalia in 1993. In all these cases, the cause of America's defeat was *ideological,* not military, weakness. The troops in Vietnam, the security guards at the Tehran embassy, the Marines in Beirut, the soldiers in Somalia—all had been ordered, in effect, to refrain from using the firepower available to them. And who issued those orders? The architects of our foreign policy.

America's armed forces are intended to fight this country's enemies. But it is our foreign policy that decides who those enemies are and how to deal with them. To adopt a metaphor: if the military is a gun, then the State Department is the marksman who decides where to point it and when to pull the trigger. The weapon itself is worthless without a foreign policy to direct its use. Indeed, there would not even *be* a weapon available if policymakers did not first make the decision—the ideological decision—that the preservation of America's interests demands one.

The United States requires a scrupulously unambiguous foreign policy for exactly the same reason it needs a clear code of criminal law: *to make explicit the process of protecting the individual rights of Americans.* A criminal code defines the actions—murder, rape, theft, etc.— that deprive individuals of their freedom and that will elicit the use of retaliatory force by government in its citizens' defense. Similarly, an appropriate foreign policy identifies the actions by other states that will be considered threats to our freedom and that will be responded to by force.

The formulation of a criminal code protects citizens not only by directing the police in making arrests, by guiding the courts in conducting trials, etc., but also by deterring crime. If a society demonstrates that it regards criminal activity with the utmost gravity and is prepared to employ the full power of its criminal justice system, without hesitation and without mercy, malefactors will think twice before breaking the law. If budding hoodlums realize there is a strong likelihood of their being apprehended, tried, convicted and punished, less crime will take place.

In the field of foreign affairs, deterring the initiation of force is obviously even more important. A rational foreign policy minimizes the possibility of war—not as its primary goal, but as a consequence of its vigorous defense of liberty. It prevents war by conveying to America's antagonists the credible warning that any aggression on their part will be met with overwhelming force on our part. If—to return to the metaphor—foreign policy instructs the military where to aim and when to fire, then it also informs our enemies that the weapon is fully loaded and that they had better take us seriously. It informs our enemies of our certainty in the rightness of political freedom—and our rejection of all the doctrines invoked by criminal-states to justify their coercive behavior. It informs our enemies that America's commitment to safeguarding its interests is unyielding.

When freedom is the fundamental interest that nations are pursuing, their interests do not conflict. If a nation holds the freedom of its citizens as its central value, its self-interest is not sustained at the expense of other nations. Just as, in a free market, an individual's wealth is not obtained by the impoverishment of his neighbor, so too the freedom of one nation is not gained by the enslavement of another. It is not an act of altruism for America to recognize the rights of the citizens of other nations and to refrain from attacking them. The recognition of rights is precisely the principle upon which our national interest rests. A free country's interests lie in being left alone—i.e., in not being subject to force—in the same way and for the same reason that it does not initiate force against others. A free country has no need, and no desire, for conquest. It grows prosperous by production and trade, not by coercion and oppression (which is why wars do not occur between free, capitalist nations). A free country's pursuit of its self-interest entails no sacrifice—neither of itself to others, nor of others to itself.

* * * * *

Individualism in Foreign Policy

The tenets of foreign policy obviously depend on the broader principles of political philosophy. That is, on the premise of collectivism, government is essentially a social welfare agency, redistributing wealth from the "haves" to the "have-nots." It is a small, and inexorable, step to internationalize the process by taking from America and giving to the rest of the world. If a productive, successful individual is to be sacrificed for the sake of other people, then a free and powerful nation like America must likewise be sacrificed for the sake of other nations.

On the premise of individualism, however, government has a thoroughly different nature. Its purpose isn't to take from the individual what he has earned, but to ensure that he has the freedom to earn it, and to keep it. Its function is to ensure that the rights of the individual are inviolate. When it comes to foreign policy, therefore, such a government views the national self-interest—i.e., the protection of the citizen's freedom—as non-sacrificable. Just as it recognizes each individual's right to exist for his own sake, rather than in servitude to others, so it espouses the derivative right of every free nation to act solely for its own interests, rather than in deference to the demands of some international collective. It acts for itself, and it acts by its own judgment. It does not subordinate its interests to those of other nations, regardless of how plaintively those nations trumpet their alleged needs. It does not feel guilty for the riches Americans have created, nor for the power those riches have made possible. It refuses to allow the failures of other nations to establish a claim upon America's success. And it does not surrender its convictions in order to placate the enemies of liberty. It adopts a foreign policy, in other words, that is consistent with the philosophy of capitalism.

Thus, the same two injunctions that guide government domestically, in carrying out a policy of laissez-faire, guide it internationally. The preservation of liberty requires inaction by government when no force has been initiated—and decisive action when it has. At home, when citizens engage in non-coercive behavior, the government does not interfere; but when someone initiates force, the police and the judiciary respond by subjecting the guilty party to (retaliatory) force. The same is true in foreign policy. With respect to peaceful countries, our government simply allows free, private trade to flourish; but in dealing with countries that physically endanger America, our government uses the military to retaliate against, and to get rid of, such threats. In both domestic and foreign policy, the proper role of government is to protect the citizen's basic political interest: freedom.

This individualist approach to foreign policy disavows any form of nationalism. Nationalism is a collectivist idea, which regards the nation as the primary unit of life and which holds that the citizen is obligated to devote his energies to the glorification of whatever state happens to declare him its subject. But under a foreign policy of rational self-interest, it is the *individual* who is the primary unit, and it is the maintenance of his liberty that is the government's sole mission. Genuine self-interest requires limiting the state's power for the purpose of upholding individual rights—in contrast to nationalism, which calls for suppressing individual rights for the purpose of expanding the state.

This approach also rejects the specious concepts of "unilateralism" and "multilateralism" as guidelines in foreign policy. Instead, the government is guided strictly by the goal of protecting its citizens' freedom—which it attains sometimes by acting alone and sometimes by acting in concert with other nations (assuming, of course, that their cooperation is not gained at the cost of adulterating the goal). It is only a collectivist philosophy that attaches moral virtue to coalition-cobbling. As is true of an individual's pursuit of self-interest, the crucial issue here is not the number of actors involved, but the nature of the goal. And under a proper foreign policy, the choice of whether to act alone or with other nations—like the choice of whether to invade

Afghanistan only with Marines or to include the Army, Navy and Air Force—depends entirely on which is the more practical method of achieving the objective that *America* judges is valid.

But simply establishing liberty as the ultimate political value is not sufficient to guide the planners of our foreign policy, any more than establishing life as the ultimate value is sufficient to guide an individual in his daily choices. More specific instructions are needed, in order to identify the means by which the end is to be achieved. While it is the complex task of political scientists to fully formulate, and then codify, the principles by which foreign policy has to function if liberty is to be defended, the answer must start with the one virtue central to the purpose of foreign policy: justice.

Nations, like individuals, must be objectively evaluated, by a rational standard, before they can be dealt with. This is the process of justice, which is the basic means by which our foreign policy protects our interests. We must recognize other nations for what they actually are in order to know how to act toward them. We must know whether they are essentially allies or enemies of America—which means: allies or enemies of liberty. The opposite of justice is: diplomacy—or, rather, diplomacy as it is practiced today, when U.S. officials simply refuse to identify a dictatorship as a dictatorship, and instead label it a "strategic competitor" with which we must maintain cordial relations. But justice does not permit such egalitarianism. Justice demands that cordial relations be maintained only with those *deserving* of cordiality. This implies certain broad imperatives for the conduct of a proper foreign policy.

(1) Pronounce moral judgment. Our State Department should rigorously judge the world's governments, by the standard of individual liberty, and make its conclusions public. Harmonious relations with all nations are not a goal of foreign policy—are, in fact, incompatible with America's fundamental goal. We only undermine our freedom when we welcome, or are neutral toward, its destroyers. The followers of Woodrow

Wilson's amoral dictum, "No nation is fit to sit in judgment upon any other nation," are disastrously wrong. We should praise those who share our values and condemn those who do not—and act accordingly. This achieves the very practical purpose of telling the world that we take our ideals seriously enough to regard our enemies as . . . enemies. It is when our antagonists are led to think their crimes will be readily tolerated by us—when they are led to think that we operate on the pragmatic premise that our interests are somehow divorced from our moral values—that our security is jeopardized. It is when they think we will never permit ourselves to be provoked into action that eventual armed conflict (or surrender) becomes inevitable. By being willing to judge others, we are expressing our commitment to the value of liberty.

(2) Do not compromise principles. Any compromise between the defenders of Western civilization and those who actively seek to extinguish it only strengthens the latter at the expense of the former. If two parties share the same principle, they can legitimately compromise on certain concretes. To compromise on one's principles, however, is to surrender the end in pursuit of the means. For example, to induce people to volunteer for military service, it is perfectly appropriate to offer them higher pay; but it is a fatal compromise to try to entice Osama bin Laden to surrender by offering to make the daily reading of the Koran mandatory in our schools. That is an attempt to buy a little more security today at the cost of our freedom, and our security, tomorrow. There are no beneficial "deals" to be made with those who are dedicated to our obliteration. Any alleged values to be gained through amicable relations with them—peace, trade, etc.—are as meaningless as the "peace" or "trade" that exists in a concentration camp. President George W. Bush had the right formulation, when he spoke of the threat of terrorism: "Either you are with us or you are with the terrorists"—and one can only regret that he has failed to follow his own no-middle-ground dictum. Similarly, there is no "happy medium" between a foreign policy of self-interest and one of self-sacrifice. The basic alternative in foreign policy—as

in personal ethics—is still self-protection or self-renunciation. Any attempt to combine the two opposites serves only to dilute the poison one is ingesting, with the result being simply a protracted, rather than an immediate, demise.

(3) Renounce appeasement. Appeasement is the pretense that there are no enemies, only latent allies ready to announce—upon receipt of sufficient payment—that their interests suddenly coincide with those of their bribers. So a Hitler is bought off with Czechoslovakia, on the premise that somehow it will no longer be in his "interests" to enslave Poland—just as it is assumed that Yasser Arafat's "interests," once he is given autocratic reign over the Gaza Strip and the West Bank, will somehow no longer include the bombing of babies and the cleansing of all Jewish blood from "Greater Palestine." There is no possibility of an equal exchange with those who can offer nothing but a promise to refrain from aggression. Appeasement is a pathetic strategy when used by a schoolboy to deal with the class bully; it is an absurd act of self-emasculation when practiced by the world's superpower. The choice to be a criminal, or a dictator, is a choice about moral values—and being showered with protection money will not persuade the recipient that his choice is wrong. It will not keep him from both taking your payment and engaging in his brutality, to the extent he feels he can get away with it. Contrary to the Marxist belief in economic determinism, material goods do not mold one's philosophy of life. And contrary to the pragmatist embrace of Machiavellianism, the only reliable allies are those that do not need to be bought—i.e., those with common moral and political principles. A killer pointing a gun at you is not someone who shares your ends and who differs only in his choice of the means by which to earn a living. The only way to protect yourself from such physical threats, therefore, is by responding with overwhelming retaliatory force—*not* by speaking softly and carrying a big carrot.

(4) Do not sanction our destroyers. The existence of any widespread tyranny, from communism to Islamic terrorism, is

not possible without the *moral* sanction of its victims. It was because so many in the West viewed communism as a "noble theory" that the Soviet Union was not boycotted economically and
shunned politically. It was because the Soviet Union was treated
as a civilized country, rather than as a brutal slaughterhouse, that
it obtained from the West the means of fending off starvation
and of procuring a military arsenal that endangered the world
for so long. Similar moral concessions on the part of the victims
have led to the growing threat of terrorism. We are often urged
to avoid judging the guilty parties, especially the governments
that sustain the terrorists, strictly by Western standards. We are
told to empathize with those who are struggling for "self-determination," or with those who need to demonstrate solidarity
with their Muslim brothers in their fight against American "imperialism." But if we hold freedom as an *objective* political standard, we cannot tolerate those who are acting to destroy it. We
dare not say, "Well, their standards may be different from ours,
but we must accept a diversity of viewpoints." We must treat
them as an unqualified evil. Yet every time such destroyers are
courteously invited to a State Department cocktail party—or are
permitted by us to preside over the Human Rights Commission
at the United Nations—America is granting them the imprimatur of a moral sanction.

What does all this mean for the *practice* of foreign policy?
Once the central value of liberty and the basic means by which to
defend it have been identified, there are two corresponding ques-
tions that policymakers have to address: Is there a threat being
posed to our freedom; and, if so, how is it to be repelled?

* * * * *

The Ideological Enemy

For much of the twentieth century, the main physical danger to America came from the Soviet Union. Today, communism's political power has faded, but a new threat has emerged. Americans are being victimized by a variety of assaults launched by Islamic terrorists, with the most deadly having occurred on September 11, 2001. The source of this danger is not simply a hodgepodge of fanatics who happen to have grudges against the United States. The danger stems from the ideology that *motivates* the fanatics—an ideology devoted to imposing, by force, the tenets of Islamic fundamentalism and to exterminating all "infidels," starting with the United States.

This is the ideology reflected in the al Qaeda disciples who faithfully carried out their September 11 calling. It is the ideology reflected in the frenzied mobs that burn American flags and mutilate American bodies as they cry "Allah akhbar." It is reflected in the Middle East suicide-bombers who readily blow up babies upon being promised eternal bliss in heaven for doing away with Islam's foes. It is reflected in the zealous acolytes from across the globe who flock to Afghanistan and Iraq in order to kill the hated Americans. It is reflected in Ayatollah Ruhollah Khomeini and in his decree that Muslims must execute all those involved in the publication of a book—*The Satanic Verses*—which dared to offend their religious beliefs. It is reflected in the existence of Muslim theocracies. *It is the ideology of Islamic totalitarianism.*

This is a creed of absolute power. It begins with the premise that total control over one's life must be ceded to the dictates of the Koran—and proceeds to the conclusion that a "holy war" must be waged against all who resist. It is the viewpoint conveyed in Osama bin Laden's public pronouncement that "to kill the Americans and their allies—civilians and military—is an individual duty for every Muslim who can do it in any country in which it is possible . . . in accordance with the words of Almighty God 'and fight the pagans all together as they fight you all together.'"[1] The promoters of Islamic totalitarianism wish to establish a world in which religion is an omnipresent force, in which everyone is compelled to obey the mullahs, in which the political system inculcates a duty to serve, in which there is no distinction between mosque and state.

Ayatollah Khomeini made this vision clear when he urged his followers: "In Islam, the legislative power and competence to establish laws belong exclusively to God Almighty. . . . Familiarize the people with the truth of Islam so that the young generation may not think that the men of religion in the mosques of Qum and al-Najaf believe in the separation of church from state."[2] The Islamic totalitarians believe that the Koran is the fount of all truth and all values, and must therefore be the fount of all laws, in all nations.

Elements of Islamic totalitarianism already permeate Muslim society, as evidenced by the dominant role of the mullahs. The "holy warriors" of al Qaeda are not gangsters, acting outside the moral strictures of their society. They are seen as heroes by the Muslim world for confronting the Western infidels. While there may be only a small minority of Muslims who actively participate in bin Laden's "holy war," or *jihad,* vast numbers enthusiastically endorse it. The atrocities of September 11 were not committed by some fringe lunatics who were denounced by the Islamic masses. There was no torrent of outrage by Muslim clerics, eager to dissociate themselves from the monstrous crime that was committed in their name. To the contrary, the crime was widely hailed in the Muslim world—and the only public outrage there was against the United States.

Thousands of Muslim demonstrators in the Philippines, in Indonesia, in Bangladesh, even in Muslim areas of France, supported the September 11 attacks, shouting "Long live bin Laden."[3] Palestinians celebrated in the streets, handing out candy to children and waving photographs of bin Laden.[4] According to a member of Arafat's Fatah Party, "Bin Laden today is the most popular figure in the West Bank and Gaza, second only to Arafat."[5] In Pakistan, merchandise with bin Laden's visage is a popular seller.[6] Among Palestinians, figurines of a burning World Trade Center and of a smiling bin Laden holding a replica of the Pentagon are distributed—as toys to children.[7] A music video lionizing bin Laden and urging the slaying of President Bush and Prime Minister Tony Blair became a top hit among British Muslims.[8] A reporter for the *New York Times*, in an open forum with teachers at a Cairo school two weeks after September 11, quotes one of them as saying, quite matter-of-factly, about the terrorists: "They are very fine young men who did this. America deserves a lesson."[9]

Bin Laden's legions of cheerleaders resent the existence of a secular, successful West, while they wallow in wretched backwardness. They resent an America in which each person may proudly assert a sovereign, inalienable right to his own life, while they labor under self-imposed submission to their mullahs. Virtually all Muslim nations are despotisms—yet the people there condemn the American government, not their own, as oppressive. This clash is not a matter of geography or "ethnicity"—it is a product of the *ideas* that the members of a society choose to accept. America is a nation rooted in certain principles. It is a culture of reason, of science, of individualism, of freedom. The culture of the Muslim universe is the opposite, in every crucial respect. It is a culture steeped in mysticism rather than reason, in superstition rather than science, in tribalism rather than individualism, in authoritarianism rather than freedom. Bin Laden and his fellow *jihadists* have taken root in that culture and want to fully implement what is still partly implicit. They are seeking to take that culture's philosophy to its logical extreme, by creating a totalitarian world ruled by Islam. They are zealously opposed to liberty—for themselves no less than for others. The free individual—free to think for himself, to act on his own judgment, to pursue his own values—is anathema to those who believe in mindless obedience to Allah and his self-declared spokesmen.

A book published by al Qaeda, *The Future of Iraq and the Arabian Peninsula After the Fall of Baghdad,* explains why, in the battle with America, the *jihadists* fear the idea of liberty far more than the threat of bombs: "It is not the American war machine that should be of the utmost concern to Muslims. What threatens the future of Islam, in fact its very survival, is American democracy." Freedom's "seductive capacities," the book declares, would "make Muslims love this world, forget the next world and abandon *jihad"* and would make them "reluctant to die in martyrdom." Muslims must therefore resist the U.S. campaign to bring freedom to Iraq, because "if democracy comes to Iraq, the next target would be the whole of the Muslim world."[10]

So freedom is to be rejected because it induces people to prefer living over dying. As bin Laden told his fellow Muslims on one of his recorded tapes: "The love of this world is wrong. You should love the other world. . . . Die in the right cause and go to the other world." His followers acutely understand the philosophical chasm that separates them from the West. One of them, an al Qaeda official, in a post-September 11 message, praised the "thousands of young people who look forward to death, like the Americans to living."[11]

This totalitarian hostility to life and to freedom is not unique to adherents of Islam. When Europe was dominated by the Catholic Church, during the medieval era, the same attitude prevailed. No dissent from ecclesiastical doctrine was tolerated and no escape from papal proscriptions was permitted. The massacres of the Crusades and the terror of the Inquisition were expressions of Christianity's "holy war" against *its* infidels. (Ironically, it was life in the Islamic countries during Europe's Dark Ages that was further advanced and less oppressive—because the Muslims at the time were under the influence of a more pro-reason philosophy, a philosophy they subsequently abandoned.) The West's dramatic change over the years has been mainly a result of the Age of Enlightenment, which upheld the power and the glory of man's rational mind. The Western world went through that age, while the Muslim world did not. Consequently, Western culture has largely rejected the medieval veneration of religion as the ultimate authority, governing every aspect of man's life. This is why, for instance, there is no mass sentiment today for making the Bible into America's official Constitution—as the Koran is officially Saudi Arabia's. This is why there is no mass sentiment for sentencing apostates to death—as is mandated by Iran's criminal code. This is why there are no Christian the-ocracies now—while there are Muslim ones. In America, even religious people generally understand the need for a separation between church and state. The Enlightenment elevated reason over faith in the Western world—but not in the Muslim world. There, religion plays the same all-powerful role today that it did in Europe in the Dark Ages.

The proponents of Islamic totalitarianism thus regard the individual's pursuit of happiness as evil. From sex to music to capitalistic profit, they wish all pleasure to be banished from human life. Toward this end, many Muslim states have a Ministry for the Promotion of Virtue and the Prevention of Vice, with reli-gion-police assigned to hunt down the sinful. Under the Taliban regime in Afghanistan, for example, the enforcers closed a new, Italian-funded 120-bed hospital and physically beat the staff— because men and women had been allowed to eat in the same room.[12] Among the activities made illegal to Afghanis were: dis-playing pictures in public places, any speaking between a male doctor and a female nurse, importing "equipment that produces joyful music," trimming one's beard—and kite-flying.[13]

In Iran games like backgammon or cards are forbidden; the books of Agatha Christie are banned; little girls, beginning in nursery school, are forced to wear the veil; and, since the chief ayatollah has decreed that "the promotion of music is incompat-ible with the high ideals of Islam," if a wedding service includes music and mixed dancing, it is broken up by the police, and the attendees—including the bride and groom—are given at least twenty lashes.[14]

In the Saudi Arabian city of Mecca in 2002, fifteen students, ages thirteen to seventeen, were fatally trapped in a fire when, according to a BBC report, "religious police stopped schoolgirls from leaving a blazing building . . . because they were not wearing the headscarves and *abayas* (black robes) required by the kingdom's strict interpretation of Islam."[15]

The perpetrators of September 11, then, were simply Osama bin Laden's religion-police, meting out punishment to American transgressors, as required by the same "strict interpretation of Islam."

* * * * *

Targeting the Threat

Philosophically, this *jihad* is a war against reason, science, individualism, progress, happiness—the values of Western civilization. Politically, it is a war against America. To win, we need to translate the danger from an abstraction to a particular. That is, we need to identify the pre-eminent source of Islamic totalitarianism today—which is: the Islamic Republic of Iran.

There are many parties eager to take up arms against us in this battle, but Iran is their impetus. It is the wellspring of modern Islamic totalitarianism. It is a nation that was founded, in 1979, by a religious revolution against a secular, Western-style state. (That it was ruled by a despot was not what motivated the Islamists, who installed a far more tyrannical government; it was the Western orientation that they found objectionable.) Iran is a nation governed by its clerics. It is a nation whose constitution insists that "the righteous will be responsible for running the country and the legislation will be based around the Koranic laws." It is a nation whose constitution calls for "the perpetuation of the revolution inside and outside of Iran, in particular [by] developing ties with other Islamic and popular movements to pave the path for the unified world Moslem nationhood." It is a nation whose government took power with a campaign of "Islamicization," in which the universities were shut down for two years so that they could be purged of the impious. It is a nation whose notorious *fatwah* against Salman Rushdie and his publishers, with a $2.8 million bounty placed on their lives, remains unrescinded. And it is a nation that has understood from the start that America is its arch-enemy.

Terrorism is *not* the essential characteristic of the danger facing America. The adherents of Islamic totalitarianism employ terrorism because it happens to be their most effective means of striking at their heathen enemy. They do not have—yet—militarily advanced nations that can mount large-scale war. Should they develop such a capacity, however—and some are trying to do so, particularly in the area of nuclear weaponry—they will surely exercise it in behalf of their cause. Terrorism is now simply one tactic in their wider, strategic offensive against the West. Iran's sacking our embassy and terrorizing its occupants, who were held in captivity for over a year—Hamas's dispatching suicide-bombers to blow up school buses—Saudi Arabia's endorsing the kidnapping of young American girls from the United States by their estranged Saudi fathers, in order to save the children from the American mothers' "sinful," i.e., non-Islamic, influence—Iran's developing a nuclear bomb to be targeted against the "Great Satan," America—al Qaeda's crashing airliners into the World Trade Center—these are all parts of one whole. These are the actions of ideological brethren, fighting the same battle, seeking the same goals, consumed by the same hatred, embracing the same malignant doctrine of Islamic totalitarianism. And at the vanguard is the state of Iran.

Iran is the ideological inspiration for the terrorists—and, simultaneously, their main political abettor. The U.S. State Department describes Iran as the world's "most active sponsor of terrorism." According to former FBI director Louis Freeh, Hezbollah is "the exclusive terrorist agent of the Islamic Republic of Iran," and has, as noted, "killed more Americans than any other group besides al Qaeda."[16] From the seventeen Americans murdered in April 1983 when a suicide-bomber drove a vehicle into the U.S. embassy building in Lebanon—to the 242 Marines murdered in their barracks at the Beirut airport in a suicide truck-bombing six months later—to the 104 Americans hijacked aboard TWA Flight 847 in June 1985, many confined for more than two weeks, with one, a Navy diver, brutally beaten and shot to death—to the nineteen airmen murdered by a truck-bomb in June 1996 at the American Khobar Towers base in Saudi Arabia—to the additional thousands of U.S. casualties resulting from these assaults—Hezbollah's handiwork has been a major element in Iran's *jihad* against America and the West.

Iran actively supports and protects a variety of other terror groups, including al Qaeda. But even if it has no links whatsoever with al Qaeda and the September 11 attacks, Iran remains our primary enemy. As was true of Communism vis-à-vis the Soviet Union and of Nazism vis-à-vis Hitler's Germany, if we want to stop the threat of Islamic totalitarianism, it is the government of Iran that needs to be eliminated. Iran is at war with America—and only America fails to grasp this.

Once Iran is dealt with, we can confront the other terror-abettors—the states that shelter, finance or tolerate terrorism. It is these governments (including secular ones) that transform Islamic terrorists from sundry, small-time criminals into a far-reaching danger. For worldwide operations to take place, over a sustained period of time, the terrorists require the cooperation of a government. They need places to hide, access to new recruits, sites for training camps, sources of financing, means of transporting weapons, etc.—which could not be done on a major scale without the backing, whether covert or overt, of the governments of the countries in which they operate. For example, the number of people who went through al Qaeda's training camps was estimated in a congressional report to be in the range of 100,000.[17] Such a level of activity could not be undertaken without governmental knowledge and approval. These obliging governments are the most guilty parties—and the most readily locatable. We don't have to send Special Forces to comb through caves and rat-holes; we just have to pinpoint the presidential palaces in those nations' capitals.

Like Iran, these enablers of terrorism must be judged as dangers to our freedom and our lives—dangers we must actively remove, not merely wag our fingers at. These states can no longer be permitted to host terrorist leaders, or to establish "charities" for terrorists, or to utilize their banks to launder money for al Qaeda or to have their mosques used to incite attacks against Americans. We need to issue an ultimatum to them: either their assistance to terrorists ends, or we will take military measures to make it end. And once Iran, the chief sponsor of terrorism, is done away with, the lesser ones—Syria, Saudi Arabia, Libya, Sudan—will likely be deterred. Their rulers will cease supporting terrorism once they are fully convinced that they will not be around for long if they don't.

Carrying out such a policy, though, requires moral confidence. It requires the conviction that we have the right, and the responsibility, to use force against threats to our liberty, irrespective of international disapproval. It is relatively easy for our officials to take military measures against al Qaeda; apart from Libertarians and hard-core leftists, who insist that America invited attack by its "overbearing" foreign policy, virtually no one in the West excuses Osama bin Laden's evils. Somewhat stronger political resolve is required to tackle al Qaeda's sundry comrades-in-terrorism, such as Islamic Jihad, Hamas and Hezbollah, since their acts of butchery have not been quite spectacular enough to galvanize world opinion against them. But it is when they must confront state sponsors of terrorism that our policymakers are hopelessly paralyzed. That is when flocks of distraught diplomats emerge to argue that nothing drastic can be done. America cannot "isolate" itself from such countries, they declare. We cannot threaten them—we have to operate within the spirit of cooperation—we cannot breach international protocol—we have to find some "mutually beneficial" compromise—we cannot unilaterally pursue our interests. So we cling to the conceit that diplomacy will keep us safe.

This dismal, appeasing approach is pursued with particular zeal when we deal with certain types of despots—those we wish to laud as "allies." Now, one can morally justify cooperating with a statist nation that is helping us deter a significant peril (though it should not be considered a friend, but an ad hoc partner). That is, one can justify cooperating with a pickpocket for the purpose of apprehending a mass murderer—but only under two conditions. First, the pickpocket must not be in cahoots with the murderer. Second, one must not help the pickpocket pretend he is a saint. But America compliantly accepts the absence of both these conditions in dealing with many of its alleged allies in the war against terrorism.

Saudi Arabia is an obvious illustration. The Saudi government has refused to allow American officials to interview families of the September 11 hijackers; it rewards the families of suicide-bombers, including those who have killed Americans; it funnels money into al Qaeda's coffers; and it finances an array of Wahhabi indoctrination schools, or *madrasas,* where new crops of Islamic holy-warriors are continually cultivated, both inside and outside Saudi Arabia. Yet it is deemed an ally in our war against terrorism. Further, we obsequiously persist in describing that nation as a "moderating" force rather than a repressive regime. For example, it officially calls for the beheading of apostates, it forbids Jews from setting foot on its soil, it prohibits Christian worship—yet our State Department refuses to include Saudi Arabia in a list it is legally required to maintain of countries that seriously violate religious freedom. It is bad enough that we will not acknowledge which nations are our enemies; but our readiness to grant them a moral endorsement is utterly perverse.

* * * * *

The Policy of Appeasement

Even the very worst of our enemies—Iran—receives our moral endorsement. Our government meekly treats Iran like a respectable, civilized nation, whose good will we must diligently nourish. When the U.S. hostages held by Tehran during the 1979 embassy takeover filed a civil lawsuit against Iran for monetary damages, the (second) Bush administration entered the court proceedings—to have the suit *dismissed.* Claiming that "national foreign policy interests are at stake," the Justice Department argued that we should abide by the "agreement, " reached upon the release of the captives, under which we absolved Iran of all legal liability for its crime.[18] Our government is apparently concerned that if we go back on our word—a word extorted at gunpoint by a barbarous kidnapper—the criminal would accuse us of lacking moral scruples. So we penalize the earliest American victims of Iranian savagery—in order to maintain the diplomatic illusion that we are dealing with a rational nation.

In a further effort to placate Tehran, Secretary of State Colin Powell refused to give even a nod of approval to the Iranians who staged public demonstrations against their theocratic state. Instead, Mr. Powell declared: "The best thing we can do right now is not get in the middle of this family fight too deeply."[19] He apparently wants to assure the ayatollahs that we regard their power to imprison and execute anyone who criticizes them as simply their means of handling a mild spat among family members.

Our appeasing attitude toward Iran was begun in 1979 by Jimmy Carter, with his timid reaction to the hostage-taking; it was continued by Ronald Reagan, with his sale of arms to the ayatollahs in a bizarre attempt to obtain their help in gaining the release of American hostages in Lebanon (who were being held by Iran's bosom ally, Hezbollah); and it remains in place under George W. Bush. Immediately after September 11, according to the *New York Times*, a senior Bush administration official "thanked Iran for its condolences and asked for its cooperation against terrorism."[20] This craven action—the equivalent of appealing to Hitler for help in fighting anti-Semitism—is the quintessence of morally sanctioning one's destroyers.

If self-interest were the premise driving our foreign policy, we would identify the nature of the threat to America and decide to eradicate it—by using whatever force is required. Instead, it is the premise of self-sacrifice that prompts Washington to deal with our enemies through the feeble tactic of conciliation. It is the various versions, religious and secular, of the self-effacing maxim "Judge not, that ye be not judged" that keep us from standing up for our ideas. Moral self-doubt infects our entire foreign policy. Because our officials are uncertain about the moral validity of America's war on terrorism, they frantically plead for approval—from the Islamic world that holds bin Laden in such high regard. When the Bush administration decided to remove the Taliban from power in Afghanistan, it felt compelled to demonstrate that it was not out to destroy all Muslims. Instead of assuming that any Muslims who opposed bin Laden's *jihad* would be eager to convince America that they are not its enemies, the administration felt that the onus of proof was on its shoulders.

Among its ingratiating efforts, designed to convey the message that America's system of capitalism is benign to peaceful Muslims, were: the distribution, to Islamic nations, of a video documentary depicting Muslims who said they were living happily in America; the creation of a forum "to encourage dialogue" between young American and young Arab viewers of MTV; the production of a tape of a Muslim imam delivering the invocation to Congress; the printing of posters titled "Mosques in America"; and the issuing of an invitation to 50 Muslim ambassadors to break the Ramadan fast in the White House.[21] To further show our sensitivity to Muslim concerns, Operation Infinite Justice, the original name of the military invasion of Afghanistan, was discarded after Muslims complained that "infinite justice" is something only Allah can achieve. All these fawning attempts accomplished nothing except to project America's moral uncertainty in this battle and thereby to vitalize our enemies.

President Bush was incapable of simply declaring to Muslims: "America values freedom; your countries do not; choose which side you prefer." He couldn't do that, because he lacked the *intellectual* conviction in the rightness of our political principles—a failing of which the entire West is guilty. When one Western leader, Italian prime minister Sylvio Berlusconi, actually tried to make such a statement, he quickly retreated in the face of philosophical opposition. Two weeks after September 11, he uttered a plain truth: "We should be confident of the superiority of our civilization, which consists of a value system that has given people widespread prosperity in those countries that embrace it and guarantees respect for human rights and religion. This respect certainly does not exist in Islamic countries." This "politically incorrect" statement was denounced by virtually everyone, from the European Union to the Arab League—whereupon Mr. Berlusconi issued a humble apology: "I'm sorry that some of my words, interpreted wrongly, could have hurt my Arab and Muslim friends."[22]

This moral self-doubt is so pervasive that the American government docilely agrees to restrict the freedom of its own citizens in order to pacify its terror-assisting "allies." For example, Saudi Arabia forbids the distribution of non-Wahhabi religious material, and the U.S. government actively implements this oppression. The Postal Service is not allowed to deliver to American soldiers in Saudi Arabia any material, like a Bible, that is "offensive" to the religious authorities there. Similarly, the U.S. Consulate banned a Catholic mass on consular premises, in deference to Saudi sensibilities. In a further enforcement of religious controls, any female soldier in Saudi Arabia who tries to travel off-base in a vehicle that does not have a male escort doing the driving, with her ensconced in the back seat, is subject to punishment—*by a U.S. court-martial.* (And these are soldiers who are in that country in order to protect the Saudis from attack by their neighbors.)

The motive behind such spinelessness by our officials is not something as semi-rational as a desire to prevent a cutoff of Saudi oil; America could readily take over the oilfields militarily (they properly belong to Western companies anyway, which developed them and from which they were expropriated decades ago by the Saudi state). The only explanation is that we have morally acquiesced to the Saudis. We are reluctant to pronounce judgment on them. We don't believe we are entitled to assert our own standards. We have concluded that we must compromise those standards—i.e., that we have to give up some of our freedom—in order to accommodate the wishes of tyrants.

The same weakness obstructs our dealings with our European allies. Many of them are not only failing to join us in defending freedom, but are openly supporting our enemies. Anti-Americanism is on the rise in Europe, as it was during the 1970s and 1980s, when the streets were filled with demonstrations against U.S. "militarism" because then too we did not choose disarmament as our response to a totalitarian threat. Yet, while we may issue a short-lived scolding to, say, France, we refuse to consider harsher measures. We refuse to inform the European countries that if there is to be cooperation between us, it will be by our standards or not at all—that they must make the stark choice between backing the terrorist-totalitarian axis and backing America—that we have not changed sides over the years in the battle between freedom and its enemies, but if they have, then they must start fending for themselves. Instead, we continue to endure the hostility of the Europeans, while providing the military defense that has kept them safe in this dangerous world.

A corollary of the unwillingness to make discriminating moral judgments among nations is the eagerness to make egalitarian declarations of moral equivalence. During the Cold War, the advocates of arms control believed that nuclear weapons in Soviet hands and in American hands constituted the same danger, and that our safety required that both arsenals be equally limited.

Our officials evaded the fact that Soviet arms were the means of destroying freedom while American arms were the means of defending it. So they sought, not the solid shield of military superiority, but the sham security of "Mutual Assured Destruction." Today, too, we want to control "nuclear proliferation," but without distinguishing between free nations and dictatorships. For example, the director of the United Nations' International Atomic Energy Agency, with which we collaborate, says that the way to keep nuclear weapons out of the hands of aggressor-states is for all nations, including the United States, to disarm: "We must abandon the unworkable notion that it is morally reprehensible for some countries to pursue weapons of mass destruction yet morally acceptable for others to rely on them for security."[23]

Our foreign policy's most egregious display of moral egalitarianism, though, is in its approach toward Israel and the Palestinians. Instead of coming out categorically in support of the Israelis, America is driven by a need to a find moral equivalence between the two parties. (And the fact that America is regarded by most of the world as being too "biased" toward Israel shows only how biased the world is against non-egalitarianism—i.e., justice.) In the entire Middle East, there is only one free country: Israel. In the rest of that region—from the feudal monarchy of Saudi Arabia to the socialist dictatorship of Syria to the autocracy called the Palestinian Authority—the people live as serfs. While Israel is a mixture of freedom and government controls, it is a blooming oasis of liberty when compared with the surrounding desert of despotism. Unlike all its neighbors, Israel recognizes individual rights. This fact, not any ethnic or religious "birthright," is what gives the state of Israel its legitimacy. Its inhabitants, including Arabs, can criticize the government without facing imprisonment or beheading. There is freedom of the press, with private ownership and private opinions flourishing. There are unlimited political parties and free elections, as a result of which the parliament includes Arabs and even pro-Palestinian parties. *None* of this exists in the surrounding nations. This alone should reveal the nature of the two sides in the conflict. Yet our policy is to demand "equal" concessions. We are unwilling to judge one side as morally right and the other as morally wrong.

People have a right to form a government to enable themselves to live in freedom. But they have no right of "self-determination" to establish a dictatorship—which is what the Palestinians are demanding. Since the life of the individual, rather than the glorification of the tribe, is the appropriate moral standard, the crucial question is not which ethnic group runs the government, but what rights the individual is able to exercise. And by that standard, an Arab who lives in Israel enjoys far greater freedom than he would in any other Middle East country, including a new Palestinian state. Yet most Palestinians seem to prefer living in a prison, as long as the jailers are their ethnic brothers. If and when the Palestinians reject the rule of force, if and when they accept a system of individual rights and oust Arafat and his spiritual henchmen—if and when they show that they want to live under a system that is as free as Israel's—then one can talk about the propriety of creating a Palestinian state. But not before. And in regard to those Palestinians who do care about their actual freedom and not their "collective identity"—who is noticing that *their* rights are being violated when they are made to live under the jurisdiction of the Palestinian Authority rather than of Israel?

As to the question of occupied territory, a free nation that is invaded has every right to take over the lands of the attacker, should it so choose. It has the right to do whatever is necessary to ensure its own safety, and the aggressor state has no right to demand otherwise. Thus Israel is entitled to occupy, or even annex, the land on which the Palestinian problem now exists—and from which attacks against Israel were launched, when the territory was under Egyptian and Jordanian rule.

America should stop the shameful policy of "even-handedness" in the Middle East conflict. The proper resolution of a battle between advocates of freedom and advocates of statism is not for the former to compromise their values, but for the latter to abandon theirs. In our war against terrorism, Israel is our most reliable ally—and the one we treat most unjustly. To pronounce the moral judgment that Israel is pro-freedom and that its Arab foes are not, is to further our own interests. Because Israel is a bastion of Western civilization, its primary enemy, like ours, is Islamic totalitarianism. The more successful Israel is in *its* war, therefore, the more successful we will be in ours.

* * *

While the principal danger we face comes from the Islamic world, there are other dangers as well—dangers that are likewise being fostered by our conciliatory foreign policy. In dealing with the most immediate of these—North Korea's nuclear capacity—we are practicing a particularly odious form of conciliation: overt payoffs.

The communist state of North Korea, which is on our government's list of major sponsors of terrorism, has long been hostile to America. For over a decade, we have been aware of its efforts to develop a nuclear bomb. And for the past decade, we have been entrusting our security to a vicious dictator's promise that he would not produce nuclear weapons. In exchange for that promise, we agreed to help keep his totalitarian regime functioning. We supplied him with food and with power plants, so that he could sustain the populace that his policies had rendered destitute.

When it became known that North Korea was violating the agreement, by producing weapons-grade plutonium and by acquiring long-range missile technology, the U.S. government got tough—by insisting on another treaty, under which North Korea would again vow to stop being a danger to us. But this time, we were told, the treaty would "work." Of course, a treaty that will work requires far more bribery, to gain North Korea's consent, than did a treaty that didn't work. So negotiations are under way—with the involvement of four other countries, as a demonstration of our "multilateralist" inclinations—to determine the extent of the new concessions we will have to make.

If self-interest were our guiding principle, we would realize the senselessness of yielding to this shakedown racket. For we are telling North Korea that whenever it wants something more from us, it need only rattle its nuclear saber and we will be there with open checkbooks. We are announcing our acceptance of unending extortion.

If self-interest were our guiding principle, we would have treated North Korea strictly as a military problem, requiring a military solution. We would have emulated the Israelis, who acted unilaterally in 1981 to destroy an uncompleted Iraqi nuclear reactor that was designed to make possible the production of atomic weapons. Israel did not ask for U.N. permission; it did not seek approval to send in inspectors; it did not assemble a coalition; it did not ask Saddam Hussein how much money would be needed to induce him to stop. It simply decided that it had objective evidence of a pending threat from a dictatorial state—and acted to remove it. That decision was the model we could have followed in dealing with North Korea—certainly, ten years ago, when the danger was in its embryonic stages. But that would have been too self-assertive for us. The catechism of compromise demands that we resolve our problems by considering the other point of view and by giving the opposing party a chance to participate in the give-and-take of negotiations. It demands that we not focus solely on our own interests.

When the world's wealthiest and strongest nation allows itself to be put in the ludicrous position of paying protection money to a backward country, whose people regularly die of starvation—it is clear that self-interest is not the payer's guiding principle.

* * * * *

The Shackles of Self-Sacrifice

Predictably, when our policymakers *do* occasionally decide to use force to remove a threat, they undermine themselves by acts of self-sacrifice. When we invaded Afghanistan, our aim was to eliminate the danger to us posed by the Taliban. But, to avoid appearing "insensitive" to the needs of others, we then subordinated that goal to other, conflicting considerations. For example, we curtailed our military operations on the first Friday—an Islamic holy day—of the campaign, in deference to the feelings of Muslims. Our officials further debated whether to scale back our efforts during the subsequent holy month of Ramadan ("It is a very important religious period, and we will take that into account," Secretary Powell said.[24]) To show our concern for the local citizenry, we had our soldiers drop food packages prior to the fighting—food that also went to feed the Taliban and their followers.

We were apologetic to the Afghanis for taking the military measures necessary to annihilate their enslavers. As described in the *New York Times*: "Americans have generated anger by searching homes and wrongly arresting people, said Hajji Azrat Khan, an elder of the Ahmadzai tribe who lives not far from the American base in Gardez. This problem—offended local sensibilities—also exists in Iraq." And what have we been doing about this problem? We have tried to mollify those "sensibilities." In Afghanistan, the *Times* reports, "The task of reversing this kind of sentiment quickly has fallen to a Provincial Reconstruction Team, essentially a civil affairs unit of about 60 American soldiers whose focus is less on capturing terrorists than on winning public support." How? By ingratiating themselves with the populace through repairing schools and soccer fields. And what do our other, *real* soldiers see as their mission in Afghanistan? "The American soldiers' role, they said, comes down to this: to fire back when someone fires at them, and then to serve as de facto bodyguards for the reconstruction team."[25]

With our troops transformed into international social workers, and into bodyguards for those social workers, is it surprising that, after more than two years of military operations against a primitive enemy in Afghanistan, they have still not crushed the Taliban?

This moral impotence is even more pronounced in our military action against Iraq. Since Iraq, unlike Afghanistan, was not directly involved in September 11, the decision to invade it aroused far more opposition to U.S. "unilateralism." The Bush administration came up with an assortment of explanations for its decision to remove Hussein—but could not isolate the sole, non-altruistic justification: protecting *America's* safety.

With regard to dictatorships generally, none has a claim to legitimacy. None has a right to exist. Each functions by initiating force, and any free country has the moral right to overthrow it. (Should every dictator then be in perpetual fear of being invaded by the exponents of freedom? Absolutely. And if this premise runs counter to the U.N. charter—well, that is just one more reason for repudiating that disgraceful organization.) Whether any particular free country chooses to *exercise* that right is a separate issue. There is no reason to send American troops into danger in order to remove every dictatorship on earth. There needs to be a threat to our own citizens before military action is called for. However, if the government in question has, or is actively seeking to acquire, the capacity to endanger the U.S., and has shown a willingness to use it—then it is an objective threat and military action is warranted.

Iraq, therefore, *was* a threat to us—not nearly the threat presented by some other nations, but a threat nonetheless. Because Hussein was hostile to America (he fought us in the 1991 Gulf War, and his was the only Middle East country not to offer even a perfunctory condemnation of the September 11 attacks), his military capabilities were a potential danger to us. He was trying to develop nuclear weaponry since at least the early 1980s (his plans were disrupted in 1981, when Israel destroyed his nuclear facility near Baghdad, and again in 1991, as a result of the Gulf War). He possessed biological and chemical weapons of mass destruction (WMD), some of which he used against internal and external enemies in the 1980s. He invaded Kuwait in 1990, threatening America's access to that country's oil supplies. He harbored terrorists, like Abu Nidal, who had murdered Americans. He gave monetary rewards to families of Middle East suicide-bombers (whose victims included American citizens). He tried to have the first President Bush assassinated in 1993. These are sufficient grounds—*any single one of these is sufficient*—to get rid of Hussein's regime.

Any dictator who at one time possessed WMD must be assumed—absent conclusive evidence to the contrary—still to have them. To assume otherwise would be inexcusably irresponsible. But even this consideration is a marginal one with respect to Hussein. Even had he never possessed any WMD, the fact that he sought to obtain them and would have been willing to use them against America—whether on his own or through third-party terrorists—is enough. Just as the police must immediately arrest someone who is discovered to be inquiring about buying machine guns, our military does not need to wait until after an enemy's weapons have been fired. Once the guilty party has taken some action with criminal intent, there exists a demonstrable threat which must be pre-empted.

One can certainly argue that instead of going after Iraq, we should have targeted nations that place us in far greater peril, such as Iran or North Korea. But the overwhelming opposition to the war against Iraq comes from those who have disqualified themselves from making such an argument. These are the people who hail the use of the U.S. military in altruistic campaigns in Liberia or Haiti or Kosovo, where no danger to us exists, but who decry its use in ousting a government that threatens us and replacing it with one that doesn't. Had we sent our forces to Iraq, not for our own ends but solely at the behest of the United Nations, wouldn't all the protestors vanish? Had Hussein done nothing that could be considered threatening to us—had he been openly friendly toward America—wouldn't these critics then praise a U.S. invasion as a self-sacrificial rescue of the Iraqis from a fascist tyrant? The condemnation from this camp amounts to the grotesque view that we should deploy our troops only if we derive no tangible benefit from doing so—i.e., that self-interest debars us from taking military action.

Freedom is the state of being free from the threat of force. Because of the potential danger from Hussein, Americans were less free while he wielded power. Had our political leaders concentrated on this fact, they would have been able to make a moral case for invading Iraq, on the grounds of self-defense. But properly implementing the right of *self*-defense depends upon upholding the justness of *self*-interest. And our officials were unable to do so. They felt a need to come up with altruistic reasons—a need to show that we were acting not for ourselves but for others, that we were relying not on our own judgment but on that of a conglomeration of nations. We entered Iraq shackled by that contradiction. We were prepared to sacrifice our military values in order to secure Iraqi, and world, approval. We called the invasion "Operation Iraqi Freedom," rather than "Operation American Safety." Our forces were instructed to try to spare the Iraqi infrastructure, such as phone lines, power plants and TV transmission towers, despite the military benefit of destroying such targets; even Iraqi military equipment was off-limits if it was near what the United Nations deemed a "historic site." Our troops were ordered not to destroy mosques, even if enemy fire was coming from them. They were told to protect Iraqi civilians even at the cost of making themselves more vulnerable. "We're more likely to take a little bit more risk ourselves than to bring the population in harm's way," said the chairman of the Joint Chiefs of Staff.[26] Here is the stark meaning of this constraint, as described by a *New York Times* reporter, who interviewed two Marines: "[T]hey were most frustrated by the practice of some Iraqi soldiers to use unarmed women and children as shields against American bullets. They called the tactic cowardly but agreed that it had been effective. Both Sergeant [Eric] Schrumpf and Corporal [Mikael] McIntosh said they had declined several times to shoot at Iraqi soldiers out of fear they might hit civilians."[27]

We did whatever it took, including jeopardizing our own troops, to show how selfless we could be in Iraq. We allowed Hussein to make Americans feel responsible for the deaths caused by his own evil. We let ourselves be neutralized by his saying, in effect: "My soldiers will fire at you to preserve my dictatorship, and if you fire back, I will make sure that Iraqi civilians are killed." After Hussein's government was toppled, we refrained from disarming a prominent cleric's private militia, even after it had fatally attacked American troops; we did not want to anger the Shiites. We allowed gun-toting Hussein-supporters to incite crowds to take up arms against Americans—an act that would be a crime if committed on a peaceful street in the U.S.A.—*in the middle of a war in Iraq*; we did not want to displease the Sunnis. We did nothing to stop Syria from permitting Baathist and *jihadist* killers to cross its borders to fight Americans in Iraq; we did not want to upset any other Arab nations.

In March 2004, before being deployed in the pro-Hussein "Sunni Triangle" region, a contingent of Marines took a crash course in "cultural training." According to an Associated Press account, the Marines "were hoping to lull Fallujah . . . into a state of well-being by passing out $540 million in rebuilding funds, and showing off a more educated attitude about Arab sensitivities than they believed their U.S. Army predecessors displayed." Further, "the normally clean-shaven Marines were also told to grow mustaches in an attempt to win over Iraqis who see facial hair as a sign of maturity. 'We did it basically to show the Iraqi people that we respect their culture,' said Lance Cpl. Cristopher Boulwave."[28] The city of Fallujah, of course, is where four American civilians were brutally killed and mutilated by savage hordes, several weeks later, to the accompaniment of cheering crowds and rolling video cameras. Whereupon we launched a moderate military response against the perpetrators, but quickly aborted it in favor of a cease-fire and a "negotiated settlement"—we did not, after all, want to be accused of insensitivity to the needs of others.

The mustaches, the money, the cease-fires, the compromises—all such acts of appeasement *cause* the enemy to be brazen enough to attack us. They announce that our goal is to win the war not by destroying the opponents of freedom and of America—whether they are active fighters or sympathetic onlookers—but rather by persuading them that we share their concerns.

* * * * *

America's Self-Doubt

We were even more accommodating when it came to sacrificing our *intellectual* values. Because we weren't certain of our moral right to overthrow a bloody dictator, we kept trying to obtain the blessing of the United Nations—the organization that welcomes all dictators as respected members, sustains them with a variety of welfare programs financed by the free world and gives them voting power over whether their atrocities are to be criticized. And although we finally took action against Iraq in spite of U.N. demurral, we have since invited that organization to assume a vital role in postwar Iraq—not because we needed its military prowess, but because the Bush administration wanted the moral legitimacy it believed could be conferred only by the U.N.'s imprimatur.

When we appointed Iraq's Governing Council, we did not want to "impose" our values on the Iraqis. We did not want to insist that council members actually endorse a free society—that would be too "selfish." Instead, we tried to propitiate the various tribal and political factions in Iraq by selecting people who represented not freedom, but Iraqi "diversity." Among the council members—all named by the United States—were the following incomprehensible choices: the secretary of the Iraqi Communist Party; the founder of the Kurdish Socialist Party; a member of Iraq's Hezbollah; two officials of the Dawaa Islamic Party, which endorses the establishment of an Islamic state; and a leader of the Supreme Council for the Islamic Revolution—a group, founded and currently funded by Iran, which openly advocates an Islamic theocracy and which called on Iraqis to fight America during the 1991 Gulf War.[29] That was how our political leaders proposed to "liberate" Iraq and make Americans more secure.

There is no fundamental conflict of interest among valuers of freedom, whether American or Iraqi. Both our freedom and that of the Iraqis—both our safety and theirs—are imperiled by our policy of appeasement. But the critics on the left want America to be even more appeasing. They urge us to leave Iraq and turn the whole problem over to the United Nations. They demand that, as a show of concern for Iraq's welfare, we stop trying to mold that country's future in a way that protects America's interests. But where is *their* concern for the Iraqis who want to be free? Where is their concern for the individual who wants to be able to speak his mind without being censored, and to earn a living without having his property confiscated at the whim of the state? The interests of that individual and the interests of America in being secure against a militant Iraq are in harmony. It is only if their long tradition of despotism is reversed, and the first free Arab nation in the Middle East is created, that Iraqis can begin to live normal lives. And if that is ever to happen, it will be when America, not the tyrant-friendly United Nations, is in control of the process.

America's self-interest lies in defanging Iraq. The U.S. government does not have a moral obligation to the Iraqis to make them free—but it does have a moral obligation to the American people to transform Iraq into a non-threat to them. Obviously, this is easier to accomplish if Iraq becomes a free country. The freer any nation in the world is, the better for America. A free Iraq is less likely to develop into a future threat to us and is more likely to assist us in opposing militaristic states. However, contrary to the claims of the Bush administration, freedom is *not* universally desired. It does not automatically come into being once a dictator is overthrown. The history of the world is largely that of one tyranny replacing another. It took millennia before a nation—the United States of America—was founded for the express purpose of safeguarding the freedom of each citizen. Across the globe today, individual liberty is still the exception rather than the rule.

Freedom is an idea. It cannot be forced upon a culture that refuses to value it. It cannot be forced upon a society wedded to tribalist, collectivist values. In Afghanistan, for example, the newly drafted constitution contains such laudable provisions as: "Freedom of expression is inviolable." However, that same constitution mandates that "no law can be contrary to the sacred religion of Islam"—that the government be responsible for "organizing and improving the conditions of mosques, *madrasas* and religious centers"—that no political parties may function if their views are "contrary to the provision[s] of the sacred religion of Islam"—that the national flag feature the phrase "There is no God but Allah and Mohammad is his prophet." Is it conceivable that, under such strictures, the individual will be allowed to think freely? Freedom is such an alien principle in that culture of entrenched mysticism that it will take many years of rational education before it is understood, let alone accepted.

Whether this is also true of Iraq, which has had more exposure to Western influences, remains to be seen. Perhaps its citizens will be more receptive to the concept of freedom. But certainly what they will need from the United States is intellectual direction—*not* who-are-we-to-judge acquiescence. To lead the Iraqis to freedom, whether in the next year or the next generation, requires that we "impose" our values on them—i.e., that we expose them to the philosophy of a free society. They need to be given the Declaration of Independence to study. Their schools must teach the ideas of Thomas Jefferson and John Locke and Adam Smith. The Governing Council must be instructed to eject the communists and the *jihadists.*

American officials have to be confident enough in their values to convey decisively the requirements of freedom. The Iraqis need to be told that freedom does not mean the power to install any type of government, able to do whatever it wishes, as long as more people happen to be for it than against it. They need to be told that political liberty rests not on unlimited majority rule, but on inalienable individual rights. The tyranny of the majority is no less repressive than the tyranny of a lone autocrat. The right to vote is one element of a free society, but it is meaningless without the prior framework which defines that free society.

Even a dictatorship can, and usually does, hold elections—but the people are not freer because of them. Only after a society acknowledges the basic principle of rights—i.e., the existence of a sphere of human action upon which the government may not trespass—does the idea of free elections apply. America's constitution *limits* the powers of the state, and the underlying premise is that there are actions forbidden to the government, regardless of the "will of the people" at any moment. The Iraqis need to be taught that premise. They need particularly to be told that they have no right to establish an Islamic theocracy, even if it is by vote.

All men have the innate right to be free, which means that there is no right of a majority to vote a minority into slavery. However, those who believe that an Iraqi constitution needs to treat the people as members of various collectives, so that the rights of minority groups are protected, would do well to re-member Ayn Rand's pithy admonition: "[T]he smallest minority on earth is the individual. Those who deny individual rights, cannot claim to be defenders of minorities."[30]

The Iraqis do not know what liberty is, but we do—and *we* should be the ones to build the structure of a free society. America alone, not the representatives of their religious and ethnic tribes, and not the representatives of the United Nations, should write a constitution for that country. The Iraqis need a constitution that will allow freedom to blossom. They need the institution of property rights, without which no other rights are possible. They need private ownership of their newspapers, their television stations, their factories, their electric utilities, their oil wells. They need to be introduced to the system under which the individual is protected against state coercion: the system of capi-talism. When they get the idea that the purpose of government is not to dole out privileges to particular groups, but to protect individual rights, then they will be ready for self-government. This is the post–World War II approach America took in Japan, which was also steeped in collectivism and authoritarianism.

General Douglas MacArthur, as head of the allied occupation of Japan, did not humbly defer to the judgment of the Japanese authorities. In fact, he rejected the postwar constitution proposed by Japanese officials and had a committee of Americans write a radically new one, based on the principle of individual rights. In time, Japan became a free society.

America's safety is the fundamental standard by which to measure our success in Iraq. Making Iraq free is the ideal means of keeping us safe. But even if ultimately the Iraqis cannot be persuaded to embrace freedom, they can certainly be prevented from becoming a new threat to us. Toward that end, we should issue an unequivocal warning to the Iraqis: their future government must do nothing that will pose a danger to us, or it too will be eliminated. The Iraqis may well fall back into some form of statism, but their leaders can be made to understand that any anti-American activity on their part—such as an alliance with the forces of Islamic totalitarianism—will be met with a resounding show of force on our part and the installation of a new government. (And the same warning should be conveyed to Afghanistan.)

The war in Iraq, like the broader war against Islamic totalitarianism, is at root a battle of ideas. It is the battle between the philosophy of freedom and the philosophy of enslavement. What ideas do we communicate, however, when we parcel out seats on the Governing Council to the most obdurate foes of freedom? What message do we send when our officials scramble to accommodate the demands of an Iraqi Grand Ayatollah who, seeking a one-Shiite-one-vote theocracy, insists that America immediately allow a majority to elect a new government?

We have the military power to achieve our goals, but we keep compromising those goals in order to make them more palatable—to the Iraqi mullahs, to our international critics, to the editorial writers of the *New York Times*. To alleviate the grumbling about the U.S. occupation, we are turning over full sovereignty to the Iraqis well before we have reason to believe that they are prepared to set up a free nation. To avoid denunciations from religionists, we have approved an interim constitution which says that "Islam is the official religion of the State" and which prohibits any law "that contradicts the universally agreed tenets of Islam."

Erasing every trace of their former enslavers is all that is necessary to gain the support of the Iraqis whose opinions should matter to us. As to the others, they need not like us, only fear us. Our officials, however, are obsessed with "winning the hearts and minds" of the people by treading deferentially—by refraining from employing the level of force needed to suppress our numerous enemies there—so as to accommodate even the sensitivities of those who are hostile to liberty. But what will be inside those "hearts and minds" we will supposedly have won—other than scorn for an irresolute nation and disdain for the ideas it professes to hold? Will people think that the Americans or the Islamic totalitarians are more committed to their respective philosophies? Will our enemies be convinced that we won't tolerate an anti-American Iraq—or will they be emboldened to establish one?

It is appalling that we allow Iran, the primary promoter of Islamic totalitarianism, to go untouched by us; it is unconscionable that we may be allowing Iraq—the country we invaded in order to make us more secure—to become another Iran.

* * * * *

The Impracticality of Pragmatism

This inability to defend our self-interest, in word and deed, is reinforced by Washington's pragmatist mentality, which scorns principles and morality. It is a mentality which insists that foreign policy concern itself not with abstract theory but with hard-headed "practicalities." There are no firm truths, the pragmatists maintain, only the expediencies of the moment; issues cannot be framed in black and white, only in shades of gray; our self-interest has no fixed definition—it ebbs and flows with the unpredictable tide of offers and counteroffers that sway our foreign policy.

Our leaders are thus constantly searching for some acceptable "middle ground" between America's value of liberty and Iran's (or Syria's or Saudi Arabia's or North Korea's) desire to destroy liberty. To the pragmatist, political conflicts are essentially the same as the differences between the buyer and seller of a car: the parties start out far apart, they entertain a variety of proposals, they haggle over the terms, but eventually each makes painful concessions and the sale is consummated to everyone's benefit. In disputes among nations, too, everything should be "on the table," because making a deal is the overriding goal. "Flexibility" is the pragmatist's supreme virtue, integrity the supreme vice. He rejects all absolutes—except the need to compromise.

This is why our government's actions are so exasperatingly inconsistent. This is why, for example, George W. Bush can resolutely declare to the world, "If you harbor a terrorist, if you support a terrorist, if you feed a terrorist, you are just as guilty as the terrorist"[31]—yet be able, just a few days later, to waive the provisions of the Anti-Terrorism Act of 1987 and to assert that allowing Yasser Arafat's Palestine Liberation Organization to operate in this country "is important to the national security interests of the United States."[32] Only pragmatism's view that principles are useless burdens—that consistency is "the hobgoblin of little minds" and that there is no difference between compromising on the price of a car and compromising on the commitment to fight terrorism—makes such incomprehensible contradictions comprehensible.

It is true that under the Bush administration, for the first time in more than half a century, America actually overthrew a foreign government because it participated in the use of force against us. President Bush's foreign policy is certainly preferable to what is advocated by many of today's politicians, particularly the typical hand-wringing, America-blaming, U.N.-worshiping liberal. However, if the current policies are seen by the public as the best that the pro-capitalist right can fashion—if President Bush has in effect set the outer limits on what is acceptable in foreign policy, and the political debate is then between the left's position of subordinating our interests to the international community and President Bush's position of semi-subordinating— what does that imply about the possibility of ever instituting a foreign policy that will genuinely defend us?

A pragmatic, shifting, seat-of-the-pants attempt to uphold America's self-interest is impractical. It cannot work. It cannot keep us safe and free. Only fidelity to the *principle* of self-interest can. For America to prevail against its enemies, we must adopt a conviction quite incompatible with the bromides of pragmatism: *the conviction that we are right and they are wrong.* Not that we are partially right, not that we have to see things from their perspective, not that we need to be "tolerant" of other cultures, not that we should be willing to give away something to our enemies in order to get something we want from them—but simply that we are right and they are wrong on the non-negotiable issue of whether we are entitled to live in freedom. America's self-interest can be protected only by those who understand what it consists of, why it is morally proper and what means of protection need to be employed—i.e., the means of non-appeasement, non-compromise, non-sacrifice.

The pragmatists, however, believe that there are no differences so sharp that they cannot be smoothed over by an adept negotiator. They believe that all nations have the same ends—peace and prosperity—and therefore can always resolve their conflicts by hammering out agreements on the means. When we negotiated with the North Koreans over their nuclear threat, our State Department advisors doubtless said something like: "We want something from them, they want something from us—they don't want war, we don't want war—so let's sit down and make a deal." The fact that North Korea's government wages perpetual war against its own citizens—the fact that its government systematically impoverishes the country by its socialist policies—the fact that under America's system the life of the individual is sacrosanct, while in North Korea human life is merely fodder to be devoured by a totalitarian state—these are dismissed as "simplistic" distinctions concocted by "ideologues." Our policymakers see only that two parties want something from one another, so both should be able to benefit by bargaining. As a former U.S. ambassador to South Korea writes: "The United States will demand that Pyongyang make difficult concessions. It must be willing to provide something in return."[33]

But when the fundamental goals of the other party are the opposite of ours, an equal exchange is impossible—not merely undesirable, but impossible. The terms for buying a car can be rationally negotiated; the terms for *stealing* a car cannot. The (ostensible) removal of a threat does not form the basis of an exchange. We are offering the North Koreans something that is ours—our wealth; in return, they are offering us something that is also ours—the right to be free from nuclear attack. We lose while the North Koreans gain. If that is a trade, then so is every stick-up, under which the victim "trades" his money for his life.

"Negotiation" with an enemy nation such as North Korea is not some august process, in which proposals are judiciously weighed and debated, until finally the parties arrive at a grand-scale, brilliantly elegant resolution. The shabby little secret of such "resolutions" is that they are crude capitulations to extortion, dressed up in white-tie-and-tails. The whole wretched scenario probably goes something like this: We discover that the North Koreans are developing nuclear weapons. We ask them to stop. They refuse. We say we won't tolerate their actions. They issue a tirade about American imperialism. We have no answer to that, so we get down to real business—we offer to pay them. They say the offer is unacceptable. We raise the offer. Extensive bickering ensues. Finally, all agree on a package of economic aid that we are to give them in return for their promise to abandon their nuclear plans. Everyone declares a huge victory for peace and stability—and the whole procedure starts again in several years, when someone notices that their weapons program is continuing. At each stage of the charade, North Korea is strengthened and America is weakened. This is not a mutually beneficial exchange of value for value, but an act of *sacrifice*—an exchange of value for *non*-value.

This is standard operating procedure for our officials when they have to confront a military threat. This is what they do when they promise the Palestinian Authority millions of dollars to get it to rein in its killers—or when they shower Egypt with billions to induce it to stop making war against Israel—or when they refuse to sell Taiwan top-grade weapons in order to "persuade" China, which has nuclear ICBMs targeted on the United States, not to consider itself our enemy—or when they pay off Pakistan to encourage it to be less cooperative with the Taliban. These are all cases of our dealing with threats of force by pretending that we are "trading" rather than caving in.

Diplomatic negotiation *is* an appropriate procedure— among nations that share basic political principles. For example, if the United States and Canada were to disagree about where to draw the exact border between them, diplomats could readily work out some compromise. If, however, there is a disagreement between the United States and Afghanistan over whether the World Trade Center should be destroyed by Islamic terrorists, those differences have to be settled by military, not diplomatic, means. Once we are subject to the unjustified threat of force, there is nothing to trade and nothing to negotiate about—there is only the need for retaliatory force to protect our freedom.

"Engagement" with our enemies does not make them into friends; it only makes them into stronger enemies. It provides them with the moral sanction they do not deserve and with the material support they could not have generated themselves. "Engagement" with the Soviets sustained them for over half a century; engagement with North Korea has enabled it now to brandish nuclear weapons against us.

The appropriate foreign policy toward such nations is the opposite of engagement: *ostracism*. Let these nations stand—or, more accurately, fall—on their own. We should stop sanctioning our own destroyers. We should stop helping them pretend they are moral, civilized nations. If they threaten us, the only message they merit is the same one that any domestic criminal ought to receive from the police: drop your weapons or you will be overwhelmed by force. The paradigm here is President Theodore Roosevelt's famous reaction in 1904 to the kidnapping of an American, Ion Perdicaris, in Morocco, by pirates led by Ahmed er Raisuli. Roosevelt's terse communiqué to the government of Morocco read: "We want either Perdicaris alive or Raisuli dead." There was no diplomatic "engagement," only the deployment of our naval fleet to Tangier—whereupon Perdicaris was quickly freed.

If we want to reduce the threat presented by certain nations, let us engage the people who deserve it. Let us engage the people who want to overthrow their oppressive governments. Let us lend our moral support to the Iranian protestors who want to get rid of their theocracy. Let us support the Cubans who have escaped to America and want to remove the Castro regime. Let us support the Taiwanese, who want a free China. Let us support the Chinese dissidents, such as the demonstrators at Tiananmen Square, instead of cozying up to their jailers. If we want to throw a lifeline to the forces of freedom, wherever they may exist, let us collaborate with *them*—but let us ostracize their dictatorial governments.

* * * * *

The Practicality of Principles

Defending America's self-interest requires a long-range perspective, which a principled foreign policy provides. The pragmatic, compromising method does not. It is a short-range approach, which is unable to see beyond the moment after next. The pragmatist perceives only the here-and-now, dismissing as academic speculation any assertions about the distant consequences of today's decisions. Nothing is definite, everything changes—he argues—and to raise the specter of the long-term effects of range-of-the-moment action is to worship the hobgoblin of consistency.

We overwhelmed Iraq in the 1991 Gulf War—but refrained from removing Hussein, because we did not want to displease our Arab "allies," who felt a greater kinship toward the government of Baghdad than of Washington. We confronted North Korea on its nuclear program in 1994—but allowed its facilities to remain in place, because we did not want to arouse world disapproval over U.S. "unilateralism." In both cases we allowed a threat to fester because the future—a future now upon us—was an unreal abstraction to our pragmatic policymakers.

After the USS *Pueblo* was seized in international waters by North Korea in 1968 and its crew tortured for almost a year—with the ship itself still on public display, at a Pyongyang propaganda exhibit—no retribution was ever exacted by us. After our embassy was overrun by Iran in 1979 and its occupants brutally incarcerated for fourteen months, no retribution was exacted. When a U.S. manned surveillance aircraft was forced down in international airspace by China in 2001, no retribution was exacted. Each such atrocity committed against us was viewed from within the hermetic world of the here-and-now. After all—the pragmatists insisted—we did eventually manage to obtain the return of our naval crew, our embassy personnel and our spy plane, so why upset the fragile web of diplomatic relationships so painstakingly woven together by our State Department? They do not permit themselves to grasp the fact that each time we allow ourselves to be attacked with impunity—on the belief that our actions, or inactions, today have no influence upon tomorrow—we encourage future assailants.

Similarly, every military retreat we go through—in Vietnam, in Lebanon, in Somalia—convinces our enemies that if they snipe at us long enough, we will in due course withdraw. It is not that we should necessarily have undertaken such campaigns in the first place; many of our retreats occurred where we had no genuine self-interest at stake. Rather, the problem is the prevailing pragmatist mentality that puts us into must-lose situations—the mentality that is comfortable only with the indefinite, the tentative, the provisional—the mentality of the agnostic and of the tiptoer—the mentality that can send soldiers into battle, prevent them from fighting aggressively and then be taken aback when they are routed. In Vietnam, for example, while we had the right to repel a communist takeover of that country, the crime Washington perpetrated was against the American people, whose security was not at stake and who should not have been sent to fight an altruistic war. Our government inched into that conflict in typically pragmatic form: never committing itself to a definitive course of action and blinding itself at each stage to what would inevitably ensue. First, it sent the anticommunist forces in Vietnam some supplies, then a handful of advisors, then occasional air cover, then some ground troops, then some more ground troops—then, surprised at the enemy's reciprocal escalation, Washington replied with another upward ratcheting of some more resources, some more personnel, some more bombing—never willing to declare all-out war, always hoping that just one more day or one more bullet would persuade the enemy to settle for a stalemate and negotiate a deal with us. Ultimately, finding itself engaged in a real war but unwilling to allow the military to take the steps necessary to win it, Washington had to withdraw ignominiously. This pragmatic pattern of irresolution and ineffectualness characterizes virtually all our military efforts since World War II. It invites our enemies, long after their hope of achieving victory on the battlefield has vanished, to continue their fight—as they are now doing in Afghanistan and in Iraq. It tells them that they need not fear us.

Following the 1996 Hezbollah attack on us at the Khobar Towers in Saudi Arabia, our Defense Department proclaimed that we would not be cowed into abandoning our military objectives. Here is what Osama bin Laden said, soon after, in one of his "Declarations of War" against America:

"Where was this false courage of yours when the explosion in Beirut took place on 1983 AD (1403 AH). You were turned into scattered bits and pieces at that time; 241 mainly Marine soldiers were killed. And where was this courage of yours when two explosions made you leave Aden [in Yemen, site of the attack on the USS *Cole*] in less than twenty-four hours! But your most disgraceful case was in Somalia, where . . . when tens of your soldiers were killed in minor battles and one American pilot was dragged in the streets of Mogadishu, you left the area carrying disappointment, humiliation, defeat and your dead with you. Clinton appeared in front of the whole world threatening and promising revenge, but these threats were merely a preparation for withdrawal. You have been disgraced by Allah and you withdrew; the extent of your impotence and weaknesses became very clear."[34]

Our chickens keep coming home to roost. Our use of force to defend against aggression has been so erratic that many of our enemies are undeterred. Our vacillating foreign policy has made bin Laden believe that he and his fellow Islamic totalitarians would prevail against us because we would be unwilling to sustain the battle until the end. They hold the premise that they are committed to a hallowed cause and that we are committed only to . . . a hallowed middle ground.

A principled foreign policy anticipates future consequences. It deals decisively with a small problem—like North Korea's nascent nuclear program in the early 1990s—in order to avoid having to deal with a crisis—like North Korea's possession of a working nuclear bomb today. It is therefore preposterous to hear objections to President Bush's supposedly new doctrine of "pre-emptive war." A proper foreign policy *must* be pre-emptive. Apart from the matter of delivering punishment, *all* responses to initiations of force—by police or by soldiers—are pre-emptive; they stop the next attack, whether it would have occurred in the next moment or the next year. When we declared war on the Japanese after Pearl Harbor, we did not say: "Well, we failed to intercept their raid, so if we use force now it will only be 'pre-emptive.'" Instead, we chose immediately to retaliate—and, with each act of retaliation, we diminished Japan's capacity to harm us. Once our State Department has evidence that a party is taking actions that could physically endanger us, it has a moral obligation to pre-empt that threat without delay.

Had we followed such a policy, we would have realized, far before September 11, 2001, the need to take pre-emptive military measures against the Taliban government in Afghanistan, along with its deadly houseguest, al Qaeda. Yet even now, the only concern our concrete-bound pragmatists have is why some particular dot of information was not combined with some other dot of information to give us advance notice of the planned September 11 hijackings. They are preoccupied with playing "connect-the-dots," while they remain blind to the actual big picture—the picture revealed by understanding the relevant principles, without which *no* quantity of dots would suffice. They believe that the only way for us to be safe is to know beforehand our enemy's specific means, target and time of attack. They refuse to see that the prerequisite for anticipating possible dangers is to think in fundamentals—for example, to identify an entity like al Qaeda, well before it brought down the World Trade Center, as a killer whose domicile is known and who should be obliterated by whatever means necessary. They carp about the FBI's inadequate response to some ambiguous e-mail received prior to September 11—but are oblivious to our government's mammoth, *ongoing* dereliction in granting immunity to state sponsors of terrorism.

* * *

Pragmatism's myopic approach cannot defend us. A foreign policy that disavows principles leads to the same result as one that openly calls for self-sacrifice: namely, the surrender of America's interests. This is true even of the arch-"practical" school of *realpolitik,* which claims to endorse a foreign policy that upholds the national interest.

The proponents of this school lack any firm idea of what constitutes a nation's self-interest. The closest they come is in vaguely encouraging a country to carve out "spheres of influence," to exert control, to dominate other countries. The state's interests, they believe, consist in accumulating power. But power—to do what? To attain the state's goals. What are its goals? To be able to do whatever it wishes to do. And what should it wish to do? To be powerful.

There is no purpose to which this power is to be put. It does not enforce some ideology—the advocates of this school reject ideology. They simply endorse the power to wield power—a view that is obviously destructive of the actual interests of the individual citizen, whose energies and whose life are conscripted into the service of an imperial, power-lusting state. Of course, this is too untenable a position for the disciples of *realpolitik* to advance very strongly. Accordingly, in keeping with pragmatism's insistence on compromise and flexibility, they dilute it. Power is fine, they say, but not too much. America's interests do lie in ruling the world, but not if taken to "extremes."

But this only shows why the role of morality is inescapable. In prescribing how the state ought to act, even the *realpolitik* supporters must ultimately rely on some moral justification. Their idea of an appropriate foreign policy can be defended only by arguing that it is the best means of attaining some morally defensible end. If they want to adopt a foreign policy that "works," the question must be: works—to achieve what? They must explain why it is *right* for us to exert power and to create "spheres of influence." So these pragmatic "realists" latch on to the culturally dominant view of the good, and issue altruist platitudes: "America must use its strength to assure global harmony"—"We can't act entirely on our own because the world is an interdependent whole"—"A superpower will discharge its responsibilities by taking into account the needs of other nations"—"America should rule, but it must be willing to serve, too."

This contorted viewpoint is a further illustration of why America's self-interest cannot be rationally defined once it is divorced from the moral principle of freedom. If freedom is the basic value being safeguarded, then our foreign policy can give us unambiguous guidelines: we use our power to preserve that value—and *only* to preserve that value. It is clear where our interests lie and where they don't. However, on the *realpolitik* view toward power, nothing is clear. There is no way to ascertain what our interests really are, when they are being endangered or what steps are required to protect them. What would the pragmatists advise on the question of whether we should, say, invade Canada? Well, they would reply, doing so would enhance our power and serve our interests, but maybe we should sacrifice our interests for the sake of world stability. What about the question of our using force against the threat posed by North Korea or Iran? There too, we can't forget our duty to consider the needs of others before we resort to arms. Should we send "peacekeepers" to Kosovo or Liberia? Well, perhaps that's a good idea, since we do have global responsibilities. There are no solid principles to use as guidelines. There is only the pragmatist's stock-in-trade: the admonition to fly by the seat of one's pants—i.e., to follow the whims of the policymakers of the moment, who will do whatever they happen to feel will "work." Which is precisely the method that cannot succeed in keeping America safe.

Thus, the pragmatists, who claim to champion self-interest and to dispense with morality, are able to do neither. The policy of the avowed altruist turns out to be essentially the same as that of the avowed "realist." The two camps diverge only in that the first calls upon moral principles and explicitly urges us to sacrifice our self-interest, while the second nominally dismisses morality—and *im*plicitly urges us to sacrifice our self-interest.

* * * * *

The Moral and the Practical

With self-sacrifice as the standard that shapes our foreign policy, any request for aid, from anywhere on the planet, creates a claim on our lives. Under a self-interest standard, it is not our business to resolve some distant conflict centering on which sub-tribe should enslave the other. But under the self-sacrifice standard, *everything* is our business. There is the constant pull to immerse ourselves in the affairs of others, and to cede our sovereignty to the wishes of other nations. There is no misfortune on earth, self-inflicted or not, in which we cannot involve ourselves altruistically. We can always send money, advisors, technicians, supplies, diplomats and sacrificial lambs-cum-soldiers. As long as one's heart is pumping, there is always more blood that can be extracted.

The entire world thus becomes a tripwire. Anything can launch the State Department into agonized pondering over whether and how to react. Everything is a potential Vietnam. We never know where to draw the line—there *is* no objective line. The result is an ad hoc foreign policy, as incoherent as it is unpredictable, under which the State Department lurches from crisis to crisis, oscillating between a duty to meet the demands of altruism and an intermittent, self-assertive desire to resist those demands by upholding our interests—but rarely knowing how this latter is to be accomplished.

Underlying this grand failure is the widely accepted false alternative of the moral versus the practical. In our foreign policy, this represents the supposed dichotomy between doing what is right and doing what benefits America. This impossible choice causes our foreign policy to be in perpetual self-conflict. We don't want our wealth to be drained to feed the vultures of the world, but we are told that it is a vice to place one's needs above those of others. We intensely want to preserve our freedom against all threats, but we are told that it is a virtue to give away that which one values most. We don't want to surrender our interests, but we don't want to reject morality either. The true alternative—a foreign policy that espouses America's self-interest *as a moral ideal*—is never considered.

It is time to consider it.

The dichotomy goes unchallenged because the only moral standard most people can conceive is one that enshrines self-sacrifice. But a radically different standard exists. As is true in all the other areas of human life, the proper policy here is one under which rational self-interest is embraced as the good. It is the policy under which the moral and the practical are in harmony, and one man's, or one nation's, benefit is not attained at the price of another's harm. If the very practical value of individual freedom becomes our foreign policy's moral standard, there will be no clash between what is right and what works.

It is because we cling to a false standard that we remain hesitant to assert our right to live in liberty. We have permitted the loathsome evil of terrorism to crawl to the surface, not because we lack the physical means of squashing it, but because we do not believe we have the categorical right to put our foot down.

Those who feel that we are helpless to deal with terrorism would see things differently if they shifted their focus to the ideological realm. Terrorism, like the other major dangers we face, is growing only because of a philosophic default on our part. We have chosen compromise and appeasement, rather than principled intransigence, as our method of dealing with the entities that make terrorism possible. And at the root of this default is the premise that pervades all areas of American politics, domestic as well as foreign. Whether manifested in our expanding welfare state or in our accommodationist foreign policy, that premise comes in the form of a single exhortation: the individual must sacrifice his interests and his rights to the needs of others.

If we are to be safe, this is the exhortation that needs to be repudiated. Individual freedom must be regarded as an absolute, which must be protected against all encroachments. For our State Department, this means a foreign policy whose foundation is America's self-interest. The challenge we face lies not in physically disarming al Qaeda, but in intellectually *arming* our politicians. If they truly grasp the meaning of freedom, they will readily undertake the steps to safeguard it. That is, if we can just get them to understand what it means to defend the individual's right to his life, his liberty and the pursuit of his happiness, we will have little difficulty in getting them to defend us against the ugly threats from abroad.

* * * * *

REFERENCES

1. American Jewish Committee, citing a *fatwah* issued by bin Laden on Feb. 23, 1998, in the name of "International Front for Jihad on the Jews and Crusaders." (http://www.ajc.org/Terrorism/BriefingsDetail.asp?did=221&pid=737)

2. Nationmaster.com (http://www.nationmaster.com/encyclopedia/Ayatollah-Khomeini)

3. "Muslims Love bin Laden," by Daniel Pipes, *New York Post,* Oct. 22, 2001, p. 25.

4. "Jewish Leaders Stress Palestinians' Support of Attacks," by Melissa Radler, *The Jerusalem Post*, Sept. 13, 2001. (http://www.jpost.com/Editions/2001/09/13/News/News.34751.html)

5. "Muslims Love bin Laden," by Daniel Pipes, *New York Post,* Oct. 22, 2001, p. 25.

6. *Ibid.*

7. Reported on "Brit Hume's Special Report" (Fox News Channel), Dec. 3, 2003. See also FreeRepublic.com, "Cute Palestinian Toy (Celebrates 9/11 WTC/Pentagon Attack!)" (http://209.157.64.200/focus/f-news/1025366/posts)

8. "Islamic Rappers' Message of Terror," by Antony Barnett, *The Observer,* Feb. 8, 2004. (http://politics.guardian.co.uk/print/0,3858,4854110-107846,00.html)

9. "U.S. Has a Long Way to Go to Bring Around Egyptians," by Neil MacFarquhar, *New York Times,* Sept. 26, 2001, p. B5.

10. Cited in "Al Qaeda's Agenda for Iraq," by Amir Taheri, *New York Post,* Sept. 4, 2003, op-ed page.

11. "They Hate Civilization," by Charles Krauthammer, *New York Post,* Oct. 16, 2001, p. 28.

12. "Afghanistan's Taliban Toughen Line With World," by Jack Redden, Reuters, May 22, 2001. (http://www.atour.com/news/international/20010522a.html)

13. "More No-Nos Than You Can Shake a Stick At (Hey, No Stick-Shaking)," by Amy Waldman, *New York Times,* December 2, 2001, Week in Review, p. 7.

14. National Movement of Iranian Resistance Web site. (http://impact.users.netlink.co.uk/namir/intro2.doc)

15. "Saudi Police 'Stopped' Fire Rescue," BBC News, Mar. 15, 2002. (http://news.bbc.co.uk/1/hi/world/middle_east/ 1874471.stm)

16. "Remember Khobar Towers," by Louis J. Freeh, *Wall St. Journal,* May 20, 2003, op-ed page.

17. According to Senator Bob Graham (D-FL), "al-Qaeda has trained between 70,000 and 120,000 persons in the skills and arts of terrorism"—interview on *Meet the Press*, NBC, July 13, 2003.

18. "Sympathy, Uncertainty for Hostages," by Neely Tucker, *Washington Post,* Dec. 14, 2001, p. B03.

19. "Powell: Keep Out of Iran Feud," BBC News, July 7, 2003. (http://news.bbc.co.uk/1/hi/world/middle_east/3041426.stm)

20. "British Minister Meets With Top Iranians Over Afghanistan," by Elaine Sciolino and Nazila Fathi, *New York Times,* Sept. 26, 2001, p. B5.

21. "Who Is the Enemy?" by Daniel Pipes, *Commentary,* Jan. 2002, p. 27.

22. "Berlusconi Vaunts West's 'Superiority'" by Steven Erlanger, *International Herald Tribune*, Sept. 27, 2001.

23. "Saving Ourselves From Self-Destruction," by Mohamed ElBaradei, *New York Times,* Feb. 12, 2004, p. A37.

24. "Powell: Afghan Campaign May End by Winter's Start," CNN, Oct. 21, 2001. (http://www.cnn.com/2001/US/10/21/ret. afghanistan.attacks/index.html)

25. "2 U.S. Fronts: Quick Wars, but Bloody Peace," by Amy Waldman and Dexter Filkins, *New York Times,* Sept. 19, 2003, pp. A1, A12.

26. "U.S. in Combat Under Constraints," by John Diamond and Dave Moniz, *USA Today,* March 26, 2003, p. 4A.

27. "A Pause in the Advance, and Some Time to Reflect," by Dexter Filkins, *New York Times,* Mar. 29, 2003, p. A1.

28. "Marines in Iraq Trade Training for Bullets," by Lourdes Navarro, Associated Press, Apr. 15, 2004. (*Boston Globe* online site) (http://www.boston.com/news/world/middleeast/ articles/2004/04/15/marines_in_iraq_trade_training_for_ bullets?mode=PF)

29. "Iraqi Governing Council Members," BBC News, July 14, 2003. (http://news.bbc.co.uk/1/hi/world/middle_east/ 1874471.stm)

30. *Capitalism: The Unknown Ideal* (Signet), Ayn Rand, "America's Persecuted Minority: Big Business," p. 61.

31. "President Visits Pease," by Nancy Cicco, MSNBC.com, Oct. 10, 2003.

32. Presidential Determination No. 2004-04 of October 14, 2003, "Waiver and Certification of Statutory Provisions Regarding the Palestine Liberation Organization," published in *Federal Register*, Vol. 68, No. 206, Oct. 24, 2003.

33. "Talking Is Better Than Fighting," by James Laney and Jason T. Shaplen, *New York Times,* Sept. 20, 2003, p. A23.

34. From Osama bin Laden's "Declaration of War Against the Americans Occupying the Land of the Two Holy Places," Aug. 23, 1996. Cited in Washingtonpost.com, "Ladenese Epistle: Declaration of War." (http://www.washingtonpost.com/ac2/wp-dyn?pagename=article&node=&contentId=A4342-2001Sep21&notFound=true)

Ayn Rand Institute

About the Ayn Rand Institute

The Ayn Rand Institute (ARI), a 501(c)(3) educational organization, was established in 1985 and is headquartered in Irvine, California. Its purpose is to advance the ideas of Ayn Rand (1905–1982), bestselling author of *The Fountainhead* and *Atlas Shrugged* and ardent advocate of reason, rational self-interest, individual rights and free-market capitalism.

ARI seeks to promote these principles, spearheading a "cultural renaissance" that will reverse the anti-reason, anti-individualism, anti-freedom trends in today's culture.

Ayn Rand's philosophy—known as Objectivism—holds that historical trends are ultimately shaped by philosophy. To reverse our current political and economic trends, therefore, requires a reversal of our society's fundamental philosophy.

The major battleground in this fight for reason and capitalism is the educational institutions— the high schools and, above all, the universities, where students learn the ideas that mold their lives. It is here that the battle must be fought—and won—in order to establish in America the ideal of individual liberty, as envisioned by the Founding Fathers.

Victory in this war of ideas will mean the defeat of the widely held, pernicious ideas that dominate contemporary culture—the ideas of mysticism, altruism and collectivism, along with their numerous ideological offshoots. These deadly ideas are the motive force behind the threats to freedom that America faces today.

Our goal is to disseminate a set of radically different ideas. As Ayn Rand summarized: "My philosophy, in essence, is the concept of man as a heroic being, with his own happiness as the moral purpose of his life, with productive achievement as his noblest activity, and reason as his only absolute."

ARI's strategy for launching this cultural renaissance has four key elements:

☐ Training the "New Intellectuals" of the future by providing intensive instruction on Ayn Rand's philosophy, Objectivism.

☐ Promoting Objectivism in colleges and universities and introducing Ayn Rand to young people by stimulating interest in her novels among high school students.

☐ Publicizing Ayn Rand's philosophy to the general public, via mass media.

☐ Maintaining a professional outreach program to bring these ideas to the attention of entrepreneurs, executives, professionals and managers.

If you are persuaded that it is in your self-interest to support efforts that will advance the philosophy of reason, individualism and capitalism— and if you want more information about how you can help the Ayn Rand Institute achieve these goals—please contact: The Ayn Rand Institute, 2121 Alton Parkway, Irvine, CA 92606. Web: www.aynrand.org; e-mail: mail@aynrand.org; phone: 949-222-6550; fax: 949-222-6558.

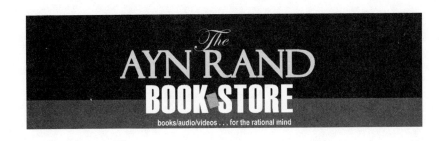
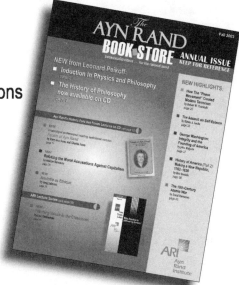

The Israeli-Palestinian Conflict . . . What Is the Solution? By Yaron Brook

Central to the Israeli-Palestinian conflict is the question of whether the state of Israel has a moral right to exist. Will the establishment of a sovereign Palestinian state bring peace? What is the solution—and which side of the conflict should America support?

In this talk Dr. Yaron Brook, executive director of the Ayn Rand Institute argues that Israel deserves—but is not receiving—America's moral and political support; that by sacrificing its loyal ally for the sake of appeasing our common enemies, America is undermining its own war on terrorism. Dr. Brook outlines a solution that unites ideas and action in its defense of America's self-interest.

(Video; 2 hrs., with Q & A) **LS023G** $29.95
(Audio; 2-tape set; 2 hrs., with Q & A)
LS023D $21.95
(Audio CD; 2-CD set; 2 hrs., with Q & A)
LS023M $24.95

Why Do They Hate Us? By Yaron Brook

America is hated by millions of people throughout the world—as is particularly evident in the Middle East. That seething hatred is often explained by reference to America's support of Israel, or the presence of U.S. troops in Saudi Arabia or, more generally, on the West's past colonialism. All of these popular explanations, however, are false.

In this provocative talk Dr. Yaron Brook argues that the real cause of that hatred lies in the fundamental ideas espoused by the people and the intellectuals of the Middle East. What we face is a cultural war, a struggle between diametrically opposed ideologies. Knowing the nature and motivations of our enemies is crucial to vanquishing them.

(Video; 2 hrs., with Q & A) **LS032G** $29.95
(Audio; 2-tape set; 2 hrs., with Q & A)
LS032D $21.95
(Audio CD; 2-CD set; 2 hrs., with Q & A)
LS032M $24.95

America vs. Americans By Leonard Peikoff

From its beginning, America has stood for the ideals of the Enlightenment: reason, individual rights, capitalism, the pursuit of happiness. The dominant trends in America today, however—trends endorsed not only by our leadership, but seemingly by the public at large—represent the opposite of these ideals. In his talk Dr. Leonard Peikoff explores this contradiction, along with our current moral cowardice, giving special emphasis to foreign policy.

(Video; 2 hrs., with Q & A) **LS033G** $29.95
(Audio; 2-tape set; 2 hrs., with Q & A)
LS033D $21.95
(Audio CD; 2-CD set; 2 hrs., with Q & A)
LS033M $24.95

9/11—Two Years Later: Why America Is Still Losing the War! By Yaron Brook

Assessing the nearly two-year-long War on Terrorism, Dr. Yaron Brook argues that, despite some progress, the war is falling short of its goal—the eradication of Islamic terrorism against the West. Dr. Brook examines the ways in which the war is failing to curb the growth of militant Islam, the ideology behind the terrorists. He discusses the situation today in Iraq and in the rest of the Middle East. He looks at the reasons for the Bush administration's inadequate response to terrorism and identifies some steps necessary for winning the war decisively.

(Video; 2 hrs., with Q & A) **LS035G** $29.95
(Audio; 2-tape set; 2 hrs., with Q & A)
LS035D $21.95
(Audio CD; 2-CD set; 2 hrs.) **LS035M** $24.95